D0494653

Accountancy

UNCOVERED

*Other titles in the Careers Uncovered series
published by Trotman*

E-Commerce Uncovered
Journalism Uncovered
Law Uncovered
Marketing and PR Uncovered
Medicine Uncovered

trotman

Accountancy

UNCOVERED

Adele Cherreson

For Jim and Matilda

Accountancy Uncovered
This first edition published in 2003 by Trotman and Company Ltd
2 The Green, Richmond, Surrey TW9 1PL

© Trotman and Company Limited 2003

Editorial and Publishing Team

Author Adele Cherreson
Editorial Mina Patria, Editorial Director; Rachel Lockhart,
Commissioning Editor; Anya Wilson, Editor; Erin Milliken,
Editorial Assistant.
Production Ken Ruskin, Head of Pre-press and Production.
Sales and Marketing Deborah Jones, Head of Sales and
Marketing.
Managing Director Toby Trotman.

Designed by XAB

British Library Cataloguing in Publication Data
A catalogue record for this book is available
from the British Library

ISBN 0 85660 900 5

Typeset by Palimpsest Book Production Limited,
Polmont, Stirlingshire

Printed and bound in Great Britain by
Creative Print and Design Group (Wales) Ltd

CONTENTS

ACKNOWLEDGEMENT

Thank you to all the accountants and non-accountants who helped me with the ideas, research and interviews for this book.

ABOUT THE AUTHOR

Adele Cherreson began her writing career in 1979 on the *New Musical Express (NME)*. She went on to edit the young women's magazine *Look Now* and to work in a senior editorial role on *Cosmopolitan* in the 1980s. As a journalist and stylist she contributed to national newspapers, consumer magazines and specialist publications, writing on sex, relationships, health, beauty, fashion, interior design and travel, as well as news.

Since moving from London in the early 1990s she has managed a team of editors in a publishing company, lectured in journalism and media studies, and has extended her writing experience to include promotional material, websites, videos, presentations and books.

Adele spent five years in corporate communications at BNFL's (British Nuclear Fuels) power generation head office and latterly worked in public relations and marketing. She now returns to her first love – writing.

Adele lives in Gloucestershire with her partner and daughter.

WHY UNCOVERED?

Trotman Publishing's new *Uncovered* series sets out to take a modern and realistic look at a range of careers, both new, like e-commerce, and established, like law. Whatever the subject, this series will give the hard facts, interesting figures, practical tips, and real-life experiences you need to help navigate your way through the maze of information on offer.

The *Uncovered* series talks about present requirements and future opportunities, as well as de-bunking stereotypes.

This book, *Accountancy Uncovered*, offers information and advice on working out the pros and cons, skilling up and starting off a career in accountancy. It's not just about being an accountant, but where accountancy can take you and what it's like when you get there.

Like law, accountancy is a well established profession. There have been accountants in one form or another since man could count and commercial transactions were made. But in Victorian times the establishment of a common tax system and finance laws gave the accountant a self-contained role. Number crunchers were given their own status.

> **DID YOU KNOW?**
> The first institute to receive a Royal Charter was the Institute of Chartered Accountants of Scotland, in 1854. In fact, ICAS was the first institute to adopt the title Chartered Accountant and is the only British institute today to use the title CA.

As accountants became respected professionals the Dickensian image of the meticulous gentleman hunched over a writing desk evolved.

Accountancy today forms the backbone of business. It provides essential services to industry, government, the City (banking and the financial sector) and individuals. It uses its power responsibly, employing performance measures and checks and balances, ensuring that information is 'true and fair'.

These days the image of the accountant is changing, and in recent times accountancy has become exciting enough to produce a new stereotype – the roguish corporate expert, cleverly and creatively bending figures and business plans to suit investors. This is partly in reaction to the US accountancy scandal at Enron, an international energy company, in 2002. This image of the accountant may be more exciting than the Dickensian one, but still presents accountancy in a poor light. Now the British accountancy profession is under scrutiny, and new laws and professional requirements are being put in place to ensure continued high standards.

Impending UK and European legislation will give better guidance and impose stricter measures on company auditing and corporate governance (control of a company's actions within legal and regulatory boundaries). This will make the accountant's role more specific and transparent and, in some instances, more limited.

Learning from the past and looking to the future – something accountants are particularly skilled at – is even more important at this sensitive time.

Accountancy doesn't feel comfortable in the spotlight and the Enron scandal has led to many changes in attitude and perception.

The 21st century has brought in a new age of accountancy with a different image and breed of accountants. Accountancy at all levels is evolving, with sharper, contemporary skills and knowledge, a real breadth of business experience, and with noticeably many more women on board.

For those wanting to enter the worlds of banking, industry, the public sector, non-government organisations and financial consultancy, a professional qualification in accountancy is an extremely useful passport.

Letters after your name are a sure-fire indication of success, learning and sheer stickability, and many young people and career changers are recognising the value of the training on offer from the six professional institutions that govern accountancy in this country.

Because accountancy and its role within organisations is so long established, the training and qualification structure for the profession is well developed. Over the last hundred years it's had to move with the times and current business practice. Nowadays education in accountancy is wide-ranging and offers the advantage of well-recognised professional qualifications, with increasing flexibility of learning.

For those training in Britain there is the added advantage of worldwide respect and recognition for qualifications gained from the British accountancy institutes. The high-quality education available in Britain encourages students from around the globe to train here and provides those who make the grade with highly sought-after transferable skills and knowledge relevant to many countries.

Accountancy training isn't limited to graduate level either. There is now a comprehensive range of courses leading to accountancy qualifications; from a degree in Accounting (providing exemptions from a variety of professional exams) to an NVQ Foundation course, the starting point at GCSE level. These are explained later in this book.

The qualifications that most people are aware of however, are the Chartered (ACA, CA) and Chartered Certified qualifications (ACCA), which entitle you to audit limited companies' accounts. Four different bodies provide these two qualifications and their roles and requirements are detailed in Chapter 7.

In addition, two institutes provide specialist accountancy training at chartered level, one for the public sector (local and central government), the other for industry.

Accountancy qualifications can lead to a variety of careers or specialisms. The two most popular career paths are practice and business.

Practice covers consultancy and client work, from the Big Four firms (PricewaterhouseCoopers, Deloitte and Touche Andersen, Ernst & Young, and KPMG), which deal with the business and financial affairs of large organisations, to small local firms that support small businesses, sole traders and individuals, advising them on tax and accounting matters.

DID YOU KNOW?
The largest of the multi-national British accounting firms used to be referred to as The Big Five, but since Andersen merged with Deloitte and Touche in August 2002, after the US Andersen and Enron scandal, they are now The Big Four.

Business covers roles within organisations, ranging from procurement and payroll to corporate finance. Employer organisations can be anything from banks and government agencies to global corporations and charities.

For those who believe that accountancy is primarily about taxation and auditing, look at what's on offer. Accountancy covers a wealth of finance and business specialisms.

Avenues of expertise include:

● Mergers and acquisitions

● Fraud prevention

- Business risk, money-laundering protection

- Corporate recovery

- Company strategy

- New business

- Business strategy

- Change management

- Litigation and financial legislation

- Corporate finance

- IT security and e-commerce

- Entrepreneurship.

For anyone interested in business (public sector, private sector and charities) or commerce (money trading and transactions), accountancy training provides useful knowledge about how an organisation works. What's more, if you're looking to climb the career ladder, accountancy experience provides a solid background for senior management.

If you are interested in taking accountancy a step further, read on for the real facts, the important questions and some interesting answers.

CHAPTER 1

Who needs Accountants?

The answer simply is: we all do. We may just not know it.

Accountants have been the business backroom boys for almost two hundred years, keeping tabs on profit and loss, checking past performance against future projections, advising on tax, auditing accounts and growing businesses.

Accountants are not only helpful to organisations; they are essential to them. All businesses are required, either legally or for tax assessments, to keep records of their financial transactions. Accountants are the people who take that responsibility. As the name suggests, accountants are those who are accountable for keeping finances on track.

They are the keepers of the company's sanity – sanctioning spend, controlling costs and driving production. Without accountants, businesses wouldn't know whether they were coming up or going under.

Accountancy can be broadly grouped into three categories. *Financial accounting* covers past transactions and relies on profit and loss balance sheets; *cost accounting* deals with current transactions; and m*anagement accounting* deals with financial planning.

Alongside accountancy is bookkeeping, which forms the basis of all financial and management accountancy. It is the processing and maintenance of an organisation's records of financial transactions. This is done in a systematic and methodical way so information contained in internal records can be used externally – for company audits and end of year accounts.

The NAO audits over £500 billion worth of public spending. Our role is to help the nation spend it wisely.

Caroline Mawhood, Assistant Auditor General at the National Audit Office*

*Courtesy of CIPFA

Until fairly recently, the accountant's main job has been to act as a check and balance in business – to be responsible for financial accuracies and priorities. It was the accountant's job to audit the accounts, pay the right amount of tax and rein in expenditure. To many budget-holders and decision-makers in an organisation, the accountants have been the secret police, keeping an eye on business spending and on those who spend. These days the high profile accountant's job is focused less on low-level financial restrictions than on the bigger picture of present performance against the business plan, and future company achievements.

Picking over the bones of profit and loss (what comes in and what goes out) remains part of the job. The more traditional accounting role (of auditing and accounting) is an increasingly less appealing one for many new recruits.

DID YOU KNOW?
Only 20% of ICAEW (Institute of Chartered Accountants of England and Wales) students now go into audit.

WHAT DO ACCOUNTANTS DO?

Anyone interested in taking the accountancy career path will be pleased to know that it's becoming more high profile, more dynamic, more integrated and just a whole lot sexier.

I advise on the business and financial implications of new product launches, marketing promotions and pricing decisions. I'm the only accountant in a team responsible for brands such as Lenor and Bounce.

Victoria Ferrier, Financial Analyst, Procter and Gamble*

*Courtesy of CIPFA

The aim of the accountant has always been to reduce outgoings, comply with legislation and develop maximum efficiency at minimum cost. Nowadays an accountant's function extends to many other requirements.

Accountants can become involved in numerous areas, specialising in various services. The main areas of work are:

- Accountancy practice (a firm of accountants offering financial and business services, advice and consultancy)

- Public sector (local and central government)

- Industry (manufacturing, engineering and technology)

- Not-for-profit sector (charities and NGOs – non-government organisations)

- Commerce (banking, insurance, financial institutions and the City).

The Four Branches of Professional Accountancy, and Some Areas of Specialism

Public Practice
- Audit
- Business risk assessment
- Corporate finance
- Corporate recovery and insolvency
- Forensic accounting and litigation support
- Client secondment
- Management consultancy

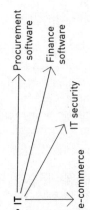

Industry and Commerce
- Financial control
- Financial accounting
- Internal audit
- Financial analysis
- Systems accounting
- Taxation
- Business strategy
- Revenue – profit and loss
- Investment
- Operations
- Sales and marketing
- Annual report
- Research and development
- Investor reporting

Public Sector and Not-for-Profit Organisations
- Treasury
- Cabinet Office
- Housing
- Local government
- Central government
- Public policy
- Inland Revenue
- Taxation
- Strategic management
- Business planning
- Financial management and reporting
- Gifts and donations
- Finance law
- Audit

Banking
- Product accounting and control
- Financial management and reporting
- Operational review
- Corporate finance
- Venture capital
- Fund management
- Equity analysis
- Mergers and acquisitions

Our turnover is more than £75 million. The level of accountability is as high as the public sector and the need to raise money as important as in the private sector.

Rebecca Davis, Finance, Save the Children Fund*
*Courtesy of CIPFA

Below are examples of the best known accounting and finance specialisms for accountants.

TAX

Chartered accountants are known for their skills in advising clients on how to run their organisations in a tax-efficient way. This has always been a key accountancy responsibility and continues to be important, with specialist tax advisors working for accountancy practices. Knowledge needed includes: inheritance tax, capital gains tax, VAT and corporation tax. Tax accountants have to keep track of changes in Inland Revenue requirements and those announced by the Chancellor of the Exchequer. It is testing work and usually auditors and tax advisors work together for shared clients.

AUDIT

Chartered accountants independently examine a set of company accounts to ensure they are 'true and fair' and comply with legislation (company law). Larger organisations have an internal audit department that prepares accounts, annual reports and finance plans. Finance staff work alongside external auditors (from accountancy practice firms) who come in and audit the organisation's accounts. Accountancy practice firms have specialists in different areas, from public health and education, to manufacturing and pharmaceuticals, to suit the clients' needs. Smaller accountancy practices audit accounts of sole traders, small partnerships and retailers, as well as tradesmen such as builders and plumbers.

ASSURANCE

Chartered accountants may become involved in assurance work which is similar to that carried out for an external audit. Assurance is part of the checking role of the accountant. This work may include: providing assurance (or certainty) over systems and controls; compliance with regulations; and e-commerce. The accountant has responsibility for ensuring obligations are met and information is accurate.

CORPORATE FINANCE

Chartered accountants are involved in mergers and acquisitions (when companies form partnerships with other companies or buy them to add to their own organisation) and buy-ins and buy-outs (when company shares are bought to change the corporate power base). Corporate finance is the more exciting end of the accountancy market, and projects are usually fast moving, demanding, secretive and challenging.

CORPORATE RECOVERY

Chartered accountants are often associated with the end of an organisation's life, as well as with its growth and development. Accountants are called in when bankruptcy and liquidation occur: it is their job to manage debts and debtors, sell off assets and tie up loose ends. However, it is also an accountant's job to try to rescue a company before it gets to that point and financial advisors are often asked to come up with a rescue package to prevent collapse. In times of economic slowdown, these jobs increase.

MANAGEMENT CONSULTANCY

Many chartered accountants went into consultancy in the 1990s and although there are now fewer opportunities, it is still a large area. Accountants are closely allied with other departments and functions within an organisation: these can include Operations, Purchase and Supply, Human Resources, and Sales and Marketing. Consultancy is when an accountant gives advice and produces plans that affect the organisation outside the Finance department.

WHAT CAN ACCOUNTANCY OFFER ME?

Because I have a family now I'm even more pleased I took up accountancy. I want to make sure I have

maximum security and the prospect of earning good money in the future. A trainee's wages are low, but that's because of the training investment an employer makes. When I qualify, I'll be earning double!
Tim Brown, Trainee Accountant, Burton Sweet, Bristol

Conventionally, accountancy has offered a secure, well-paid, well-respected career that appeals to those looking for a safe job for life. Most of those positive factors still apply, but like all professions in the 21st century there are no guarantees of long-term job security.

Staff reduction in response to the international economic climate and the events of 11 September 2001 is common to most industries and organisations. Although accountancy has been affected by fewer training places and vacancies, unlike most professions accountants have more to offer organisations in a downturn or recession. In addition, the profession offers more breadth of opportunities than ever before as the accountant's role expands.

Particular areas of accountancy are growing and there are gaps in the market – jobs in the public sector, corporate finance work, and media and broadcasting roles, for example.

The combination of strong financial management skills with practical knowledge and experience of business provides the necessary 'tool-kit' to operate in a commercial multi-disciplinary environment.
David J Kappler, Chief Financial Officer,
Cadbury Schweppes plc*
*Courtesy of CIMA

Extension of the responsibilities of an accountant or finance manager is matched by more recognition of the power and influence of the position. This means that a career in finance can be long and varied, with opportunity for advancement and greater seniority.

Although there is more pressure than ever on the accountant to be a versatile and creative business brain with excellent client skills, more varied, exciting and future-facing work is the reward.

This is my dream job, it combines my love of space matters with financial management and an international dimension. The Agency's publicly funded by 14 European governments. I'm based in Holland but regularly travel to offices in Paris, Italy and Germany.

Martin Brady, Head, Budget Section, European Space Agency*

*Courtesy of CIPFA

Train as an accountant and the world is your oyster. That's the impression you'll get when talking to part-qualifieds (trainees on their way to achieving chartered status). When they say 'the world', they really mean 'the world'. The accountant who trains and works in this country has international opportunities waiting. When international accounting standards are imposed on the UK (to be implemented by January 2005), and with a global economy and international legislation, having totally transferable skills and expertise is a real plus.

All the advantages of accountancy are based on a foundation of training. An institute qualification – from Chartered status to Accounting Technician – is your passport to any finance job in any company in the world **(see Chapters 7, 8 and 9)**.

A boss at the top of a specialist media company, a CEO of a FTSE 100 company, or a sole trader who runs a corner shop could all be accountants. That's the flexibility it brings.

Ben Joseph, Trainee Accountant, Ernst & Young, London

SOCIAL INCLUSION AND EQUAL OPPORTUNITIES

There's no doubt that the reputation of accountancy as elitist and male-dominated is justified; however, attitudes and opportunities are changing.

The Chartered status bestowed on professional accountants who achieve high academic and practical standards has always created an elite.

Qualified accountants with four of the six institutes have Recognised Qualifying Body (RQB) status, which means they can practise in the reserved areas of audit, insolvency and investment business, and this has given them exclusivity.

Two of the institutes offer specialist chartered accountancy status and although neither the Chartered Institute of Management Accountants (CIMA) or Chartered Institute of Public Finance and Accountancy (CIPFA) qualifications have RQB status, accountants with the Certificate in Management Accountancy (CMA) or Chartered Public Finance Accountant (CPFA) qualification are much sought after.

Although 'accountant' is not a protected name, and anyone working in finance may call themselves an accountant, there has been in the past a clear distinction between those who have the professional qualification and those who don't. Now there is more recognition of those who aren't at the top of the tree – the hundreds of thousands of clerical and administrative workers in finance who do essential and worthwhile accountancy-related jobs with little or no qualification.

Graduates have had the main access to learning and career advancement, but that is changing. Employers are catching on and training is in transition. Those with some years of training for the chartered qualification are known as 'part-qualified' but institutes are developing levels of their courses independently, affording them status in their own right (see Chapter 8 for details). In the future the term 'part-qualified' will become outdated and Modern Apprenticeships will be offered in a number of finance-related areas.

The CIMA offers training at all levels. In 2002 the first five papers became a Certificate, which is equivalent to AAT Technician level. It is our aim to meet the needs of the employers but also to fulfil our social inclusion agenda. Employers want the best people; in the UK employers want to fast-track bright graduates. But not everyone is capable of qualification at the highest level.

Robert Jelly, Director of Education, CIMA

Equal opportunities go hand-in-hand with social inclusion, and along with a more open-door policy on training and employment, there has been a substantial increase in the number of women joining the profession.

DID YOU KNOW?
The percentage of female members of each of the accountancy bodies increased every year during the period 1996 to 2001.

The good news is that almost half of all accountants working in the UK today are female: that's almost a third more than at the beginning of the century. Currently, female student recruitment to almost all of the accountancy bodies is at 50 per cent.

You need to be flexible and multi-tasking – that's why women are good at accountancy. I worked for a male finance director who could only focus on one meeting at a time. I had to be able to switch from job to job in minutes.

Julie Pullen, AAT Technician

There are some areas where women are doing better than others. The 2003 *Accountancy Age*/Robert Half Finance and Accounting Survey shows that in the City women accountants have an almost

42% presence. Regionally, London comes second to Basingstoke, where 47% of all accountants are female.

But it's not all good news. Research shows there's still a gap in pay between men and women, with far fewer women reaching the top of the profession, and a division of qualifications between the sexes.

- A female Finance Director earns on average £43,738 a year, compared with £52,284 for a male FD. The 20% disparity between the sexes at this level compares with salaries across all professions in this country.

- A female partner in an accountancy firm earns on average £40,813 a year, compared with £58,349 for a male partner. This difference is a mammoth 43%.

- In no area of finance surveyed do men and women have pay parity. The percentage earnings difference between male and female audit specialists, financial controllers, accountants, credit controllers, tax specialists, finance managers, heads of finance and accounts managers is in double figures.

- The percentage of women in the very top finance and accountancy jobs is disappointingly low, with more women at junior and unqualified levels.

- At chartered level, more women qualify through ACCA, CIMA or CIPFA. The more traditional qualifications from ICAEW, ICAS and ICAI are still male-dominated.

The conclusion is that although women have made some inroads into accountancy it is still the men who rule.

Many practices now involve more female than male employees; although you'll still find it's the men at management and partner level. When I was training there were many more women than men qualifying. In my working experience I have never been

discriminated against as a woman. Accountancy is the sort of profession where you just have to prove your worth and gain respect for your professionalism, no matter who you are.
Amanda Knight, Audit Senior, Richard Mainwaring, Hereford

Interestingly, evidence from interviews reveals that male employers believe women at senior level are a bad investment. Maternity remains an issue, with absence from the workplace, rather than expense, perceived as a problem. Since client relations is the most important part of a Senior Partner's job, many believe a six-month or year-long absence from client contact is damaging to the firm.

For young women working their way to the top in the profession the picture looks likely to change. Those students training now will become the accountants, FDs and Partners of the future, and given a few gaps in the old boys' network, women have more chance than ever to get on.

From an employee's point of view the bigger firms are very progressive and flexible organisations. E&Y is particularly strong on flexible working arrangements. We have part-time partners who are working mums. We don't want to lose some of our best people because they are forced to make choices. Accountancy should not offer fewer opportunities to women.
Dr Stevan Rolls, Training and Development Director, Ernst & Young

Equal opportunities for ethnic minorities has not been surveyed so specifically. Many graduates on institute training schemes come from abroad, particularly from Africa and Asia, as the quality and standing of the UK qualifications are world-renowned. However, it is difficult to assess the percentage of UK citizens of minority ethnic origin in accountancy in the UK.

Although equal opportunities are promoted through the institutes and employers, unfortunately it's easy to get the impression that the stereotypical image of a distinctly white, male, middle-class accountant, remains true.

Equally, all training and employment opportunities are open to those with disabilities. Physical impairment in particular should in no way preclude anyone from entering accountancy. The public sector in particular now offers many opportunities.

Anyone thinking of entering accountancy must remember that it is an old and in many ways dusty profession, evolving at a speed that hasn't quite caught up with the 21st century. Those women, ethnic minorities and disabled students starting out now could spearhead a change in attitude and environment, and blow some of the cobwebs away.

CHAPTER 2

The age of Accovntancy

Never was there a more exciting time to become an accountant. Because of the range of new opportunities for finance-skilled employees, accountancy can be varied, vibrant and attractive. With more convergence between business and management, commerce and industry, the international horizons for accountants with good qualifications and experience are unrivalled.

TRASHING THE TRADITIONAL STEREOTYPE

Accountants – the butt of jokes from Dickensian times to Monty Python – have never had a fascinating image. But these days the stereotypical boring grey man is being replaced by the dynamic, creative, business-focused man *or* woman, behind successful deals and well run companies.

Accountancy is going through a transition. Changes in accountancy are normal as the profession keeps pace with business, legislation, the economy and technology, but now there's a radical change in emphasis.

The best accountants are now bringing imagination and creativity to their work, whereas some are sitting around doing exactly what they've done for the past 20 years. Change is happening, but it may take some time.

Damian Wild, *Editor*, Accountancy Age

Traditionally the accountant has had two main roles: audit and accounting; and tax and legal services. Over the last 20 years these have been joined by management consultancy, corporate finance (CF) and business recovery (BR). Management consultancy has seemingly had its day (see below) but CF and BR are growth areas.

In providing corporate finance services – when one company researches the performance of another with a view to buying or merging – accountancy firms are now challenging investment banks. Business recovery has changed too. No longer does the accountant (once known as the business 'undertaker') bury a company: the job now is to rescue and turn around an organisation. In an economic climate of downturn, corporate finance and business recovery present many opportunities for the specialist accountant.

DID YOU KNOW?
In the first six months of 1999 figures from Dun and Bradstreet show there were over 21,287 business failures in the UK – an increase of 10.7% against the total over the same period in 1998.

IT TIME

The trend in increased corporate services, mirroring the way business management has advanced, has been matched by a different trend – in information technology. Accounting, auditing, procurement and finance systems have developed to such a degree that the accountant no longer has to bean-count – software takes care of it all.

We've moved through a cycle with IT. It became an important part of the accountant's education as systems were developed to support accountancy calculations and management. Now the emphasis for training is more on how an accountant can manage an IT function – which in any organisation is a huge drain on resources.

Robert Jelly, Director of Education, CIMA

With IT support, the modern accountant can spend time providing companies and clients with more analytical, strategic, creative and investigative services.

For example, the highly investigative area of transaction services came into its own in the 1980s and 1990s when nationalised industries and utilities were transferred into the private sector. Work in this area continues today but is less in demand. However, another investigative service provided by accountants – forensic accounting – is coming to the fore.

In the corporate hierarchy the accountant's role is less about control and more about construction. The finance director is no longer the brake on the company: he or she now has the responsibility of taking the business forward.

Accountants have become more influential within organisations as they have worked their way up the ranks to Deputy Chief Executive Officer and Managing Director. This influence is now felt across a variety of business functions: production; sales and marketing; and human resources.

An accountant running one of the most highly profiled streetwear brands in the world may seem a contradiction, but in order to grow the business it had to be built on solid foundations. To be creative is only one aspect of being successful in fashion. Creativity must fuse with efficiency – good internal controls, good financial practices and the ability to read between the lines.

Pan Phillipou, Managing Director, Diesel UK*

*Courtesy of ACCA

ACCOUNTANCY AFTER ENRON

The biggest impact on accountancy occurred in 2002 when the US energy company Enron was found to be performing far less successfully than was publicly declared. The company went under and the accountancy firm of Andersen (US) was held responsible for giving false accounting information and trying to destroy the evidence.

Accounting practices and business forecasts were found to be lacking, compounded by what seemed to be a cover-up job. Consequently, heads rolled, and even though it was the US company that was involved, Andersen Accounting in the UK was left with a tarnished reputation merely by association.

Accountancy became front-page news, pushing the backroom boys into the spotlight and the public got a glimpse of the powerful, influential and, yes, creative world of the accountant.

One Enron and accountants become sexy and suddenly accountancy becomes appealing as a career. Two or three Enrons and accountancy becomes notorious, negative and scary. At the moment accountancy is benefiting from one Enron.

Damian Wild, Editor, Accountancy Age

Enron may superficially benefit the external image of accountancy, but inside the profession, there is a bleak view of the scandal. The institutes have to review their own self-regulation and ethical standards to ensure they are beyond reproach, and those in the profession (especially at the top) are feeling insecure.

DID YOU KNOW?
Fourteen per cent of practice partners surveyed in the 2003
Accountancy Age/Robert Half Finance and Accounting survey
believe the continuing fallout from the accounting scandals
will blight their careers.

Following Enron, new rules and regulations aimed at inspiring
confidence in accounting have been introduced around the world.
As a result, there is now a strong emphasis on international
legislation and standards.

RESTRICTIONS

New restrictions, regulation and legislation are an impending
nightmare for the profession. Many changes are being proposed —
by the US, the UK government and the European Union. These all
contribute to a feeling of uncertainty in accountancy which could
have an effect on future recruitment and career opportunities. It's
not all bad news, however, as tighter controls mean that
companies will have more confidence in accountancy services, and
accountancy firms will be clear about what they can offer clients.

Below are some examples of current changes. They do not make
for easy reading unless you already know some background to the
issues, but it is worth knowing something about them if you are
going for an accountancy interview in the near future. Institute
websites and journals like *Accountancy Age* or the *Economist* will
have more detail, so keep an eye open for updates.

The US responded quickly to the two American accounting scandals
(Enron and Worldcom) and imposed international restrictions on
accounting services under the US Sarbanes-Oxley legislation. This
has curbed the scope of additional services that can be sold to audit
clients by accountancy practices. Now there is a perceived conflict
of interest as accountancy firms could ignore bad accounting to
keep lucrative consulting contracts with parts of the business.

The immediate knock-on effect for accountancy practices has been
the drop in management consulting business. Until 2002 this was

a growth area of business for the Big Four in particular, but it is now on a downward trend.

Ernst & Young was the first firm to recognise the potential in added services, and set adrift its consulting arm to earn extra money from management consultancy. It was closely followed by the others, except Deloitte and Touche, which in 2003 said it was going to hive off consulting, then thought better of it when the downward trend became obvious.

For anyone interested in making management consultancy an accounting career, take heed. With increasing pressure on the profession and international restrictions, going into consulting may not be a wise move in the present climate.

DID YOU KNOW?
Revenue at Deloitte and Touche increased by 33% to £1.2bn in 2002–2003, in part because it hired most of the UK partners and staff at Andersen, the accounting firm destroyed by the Enron scandal. In the fiscal year ending May 2003, revenue at Deloitte and Touche's tax practice increased by 74% to £356m, the audit practice rose by 31% to £352m, the corporate finance practice, which includes insolvency work, increased its revenue by 52% to £199m, and the consulting arm experienced a decrease in revenue. (*Accountancy Age*)

INTERNATIONAL ACCOUNTING STANDARDS

International accounting standards and auditing practices have become a looming issue in the profession as the US puts pressure on the rest of the world to adhere to its new recommendations.

The European Commission has been investigating both the effect of the US imposition and the changes across Europe needed to meet expectations and make them workable:

● The first European legislation on accountancy will be the

International Financial Reporting Standards (IFRS) which all listed companies in the European Union have to adopt by 2005.

- In May 2003 the European Commission launched its proposals on auditor oversight and corporate governance.

- In addition the Commission proposed to work towards greater harmonisation of corporate governance practices in Europe.

These measures may impose more restrictions on European accountancy practice, but the alignment of practices across Europe makes accountancy skills in these areas more transferable. Learning only one set of financial reporting standards (applicable worldwide) makes a roving accountant's life a lot easier.

REGULATION

Regulation of accountancy practice and accountants is strict and getting stricter. The institutes have always been the watchdogs of standards and ethics of their members. They apply disciplinary action and offer guidelines on good practice. Importantly, they work closely, through the CCAB (Consultative Committee of Accountancy Bodies) with government to improve the quality of guidance and regulation governing accountants.

The present aim of the CCAB is to implement government and institute plans 'to establish an independent framework for the regulation of the accountancy profession'.

It is vital to have a professional badge, particularly in the post-Enron accountancy world, where employers need to be reassured of the highest level of professional ethics and conduct that professional membership requires.
Claire Ighodaro, Finance Director, Broadband, BT Group, and 2003 President, CIMA

Responsibility for accounting standards lies with the Financial Reporting Council (FRC). The FRC puts together policy for the maintenance and improvement of financial reporting practices and is independent of the profession. Through its subsidiary, the Accounting Standards Board (ASB), the FRC develops accounting standards and issues other guidance on financial reporting.

The government is reviewing the structure for standards and regulations in the accountancy profession. With six institutes and other influential boards and bodies all having a bite of the cherry, the system for self-regulation and control seems complicated.

An Accountancy Foundation (which is due to merge with the FRC) now oversees the system. It comprises a Review Board, a new Auditing Practices Board (APB), an Ethics Standards Board (ESB) and an Investigations and Discipline Board (IDB).

There is already some evidence that the tightening of controls is producing results. The Department for Trade and Industry annual report on audit regulation from the ICAEW, ICAS and ICAI indicated an improvement in standards from 2001 to 2002.

- Of the 1,080 monitoring visits to audit firms, 91% of those inspected required no action or already had plans in place to improve their audit work.

- Eleven firms had their registration as auditors withdrawn following a visit, compared to the previous year's figure of 18.

- The number of complaints about audit work fell from 94 in 2001 to 80 in 2002.

THE EVOLVING INSTITUTES

The institutes have to both lead and reflect the changes in quality of accountancy, not merely maintaining high standards, but improving on them.

Scrutiny of the institutes' demands on members has initiated a review of all their work, from ethics to training. In order to keep pace with changing legislation and increasing regulation, most

members are now bound by institutes to continue training and
learning once qualified, even beyond ten years in the profession at
Fellowship level.

*Training doesn't stop at chartered status. Historically
once you had acquired the qualification, that was it,
now institute members commit to Continued
Professional Development. We've seen how important
it is to keep up to date – not just in accountancy, but
also in management and business areas.*
Robert Jelly, Director of Education, CIMA

The delivery of training is evolving too, with more choice at
vocational, rather than academic, level. Institutes like CIMA and
ACCA are influencing the profession and even ICAEW, the most
formal and traditional of the six, is trying to change perceptions of
elitism, with fast-track entry for AAT holders and a colourful,
contemporary look.

The real change for the institutes, however, is yet to come, as
some of the six start to merge, making their work more effective,
their voice more powerful and competition between them more
efficient. There is overlap, confusion and unnecessary jostling for
position at a time when they all need to be a strong force against
bad publicity and difficult restrictions.

*It would be good for accountancy for some of the
institutes to merge. It's been tried in the past, but
unsuccessfully. At the moment they are diluting
their own voice – with six organisations talking
individually to government and regulators.*
Damian Wild, Editor, Accountancy Age

However, whatever the organisation of the accountancy bodies,
their power and influence in the profession will be supreme, and
that's unlikely to change.

CHAPTER 3

Accountancy roles

Accountants affect the health of UK plc, that's why as journalists we want to write about them. They've always had the power and the influence, it's just in recent years their power and influence has widened, and people have noticed them.

Damian Wild, *Editor*, Accountancy Age

Accountancy support has never been more important in business and commerce. Financial accountability has become a key part of every executive's job description and business leaders have to make increasingly risky decisions. They look to finance employees and consultants to support and participate in these decisions. The accountant's job is to help those running a business understand the risks and their consequences, then manage any necessary changes.

Consequently, management accountancy skills influence every area of a business, are internationally recognised, and are valued in every organisation and industry sector.

Those that can work with internal management information, incorporating external factors, and are as comfortable with non-financial indicators as with financial, will find themselves in huge demand.
Steve Marshall, former Chief Executive of Railtrack*
Courtesy of The Times

ACCOUNTANCY PRACTICE

Accountancy practice is still a popular area for employment, with half of newly qualified accountants going into practice (or firms) in the UK. There are broadly three types of practice: the Big Four; medium-sized firms; and small firms. These provide, to varying degrees, external accounting and business services to organisations across all sectors.

At E&Y accounts preparation may be a part of what we do but it's not the biggest piece of the business. A large part is company deals, company acquisitions for example. We turn around failing companies, perform audits and provide detailed tax consulting.
Stevan Rolls, Director of Resourcing and Employee Integration, Ernst & Young

The Big Four (Deloitte and Touche Andersen, Ernst & Young, KPMG and PricewaterhouseCoopers), have the controlling stake of the work. They bring in the big bucks and their businesses in the years 1996–2000 have experienced phenomenal growth:

● The annual average income of the Big Five (Anderson was a separate entity until 2003 when it merged with Deloitte & Touche) increased by 16.6% while other accountancy firms experienced a 10.7% increase.

● The annual average growth in income for the Big Five from consultancy services was 26.2%.

- The annual average growth in income for the Big Five from tax and legal services increased by 16.5%.

- The annual average growth in income for the Big Five from audit and accounting services increased by 11.8% as opposed to 3.4% for other accountancy firms.

(Accountancy Foundation Review Board, Key Facts and Trends in the Accountancy Profession, July 2002)

DID YOU KNOW?
Salaries in the UK for qualified accountants are attractive: 80% earn more than £30k; 40% earn in excess of £50k (which in Ireland rises to 44%); and 9% earn over £100K. (ICAEW)

Corporate Turnaround Executive, Big Four
Location   London
Salary and benefits   £35–40k
Duration   Permanent
Skills The Corporate Restructuring team at this leading Big Four firm is looking to recruit an executive to its Turnaround team. You will be primarily responsible for supporting the team members on the day-to-day operations of an assignment, or winning new work in a fast moving and unstructured environment. This will involve a high level of interaction with senior members of the firm and with client management teams, allied to a strong sector and corporate finance insight. You will either have a strategy consulting background, be an accountant or MBA, and have experience of working in or advising under-performing companies.
Overall aim Part of a team winning and executing a wide range of corporate restructuring assignments, including corporate turnaround, strategic restructuring, performance improvement programmes (working capital and cost reduction), capital rationing, disposals and fund raising.

Responsibilities Assist in pitching for new business, including identification of potential clients, understanding clients' agenda and their potential needs, and preparation for sales meetings (proposals and briefing papers). Manage the client on a day-to-day basis, conducting and supporting more senior staff at client meetings. Recognise critical issues and always seek to provide insightful commercial solutions and strategic advice to high-level client contacts, often under pressure, without impact on quality or clarity in a time-critical environment. Deliver advice on tactics, stakeholder analysis and negotiation strategy, optimisation of financial and operating structures, providing genuine sector insight and displaying deep understanding of the strategic rationale for restructuring and commercial judgement. Gain client confidence and demonstrate value through advice and sector insight.

Other details Continually display technical rigour, challenging and offering ideas and solutions. Research thoroughly and accurately, and present information clearly and concisely both verbally and written. Continually be aware of client requirements, ensuring achievement of project aims to deliver maximum value to clients, answer and output driven. Produce work to tight deadlines, often under pressure. Manage small teams, likely to include peers. Understand rationale of advice being provided. Develop knowledge of wider restructuring solutions, to enhance advice to clients and personal development.

Middle-sized firms tend to be either city-based or have a cluster of practices in the provinces, while smaller firms offer their services to sole traders, tradesmen and retailers at a personal level.

● **The Big Four provide** Crème de la crème training and advancement in a competitive, high-powered atmosphere where hundreds of graduates are recruited each year. You'll have the comfort of lots of trainee support and even organised events. You'll work in large teams of peers and specialists. There's also the opportunity to experience a variety of industry sectors (at international level) and a collection of specialisms. This is where accountancy kudos lies.

- **Middle-sized firms offer** access to large clients and a variety of work, plus increased accessibility of senior partners and managers. These firms can be found in cities and large towns and may have branches specialising in different services, so there may be the opportunity to move around in an area and experience different sections of accountancy.

- **Smaller firms offer** more personal contact with clients and senior employees, the chance to experience a job from start to finish and a high level of responsibility at an early stage with the opportunity for input and involvement.

I enjoy practice accountancy because it is very varied. I am interested in how businesses develop. In a small practice I get a lot of exposure to a variety of businesses in a short space of time. I might be dealing with a farmer's accounts on a Monday and a retail shop on a Tuesday. It's fascinating dipping into different industries and meeting different personalities.

Amanda Knight, Audit Senior, Richard Mainwaring, Hereford

Assistant Management Accountant
Location   South Yorkshire
Salary and benefits   Up to £19k + Study + Benefits
Skills This is an exceptional business with a portfolio of 'blue chip' clients. They are currently looking to expand their Doncaster-based department with the recruitment of a motivated and suitably experienced Assistant Accountant. The successful candidate will be part-qualified CIMA/ACCA (preferably at the intermediate level), with at least 2 to 3 years' management and financial accounting experience. Key responsibilities will include the preparation of monthly management accounts and associated packs, periodic financial accounting and balance sheet control. The ideal applicant will also be expected to support the Financial Director and carry out various ad hoc projects in the business.

The advantages of accountancy practice are:

- Excellent training and skills development opportunities

- Internationally transferable skills

- The opportunity to specialise in different areas of accountancy

- Once qualified and with experience, you'll have the flexibility to move to other sectors

- Good pay and terms and conditions once qualified

- Varied and challenging clients – lots of people contact

- The opportunity to stay abreast of advances and changes in business practice

- In the larger firms, fast-moving, exciting work.

The disadvantages of accountancy practice are:

- Age – accountancy is quite an old profession and you won't progress far in a firm until you are 25+

- Elitism – if you don't make the grade, you don't progress

- High competition for trainee places and vacancies

- Pressure to stay ahead of the rest and to keep up with the work; at times it's very stressful

- Changing roles and specialisms – you have to be willing to change direction and move, especially in larger firms

- Liability – practice accountants bear the brunt of legal and ethical accountability, and in the present atmosphere of scrutiny and increasing restrictions, this can add a lot of pressure to the job

- The vagaries of the market – practices have to respond very quickly to the changing business environment, and that may mean redundancies. Firms are no longer as secure as they were.

Practice still has an important role but divisions are breaking down and industry is doing a lot more itself. Working for a firm is now seen as less dynamic than it was, and people are aware of the liabilities. There is declining appeal of partner status and most trainees in large firms want to be entrepreneurs.
Damian Wild, Editor, Accountancy Age

The internal structure of an accountancy practice differs according to the size of firm and the services it offers. The diagram on the next page shows an example of the hierarchy of a medium-sized firm.

PUBLIC SECTOR AND NOT-FOR-PROFIT

For those whose interests lie in the UK and in particular in the running of central, devolved and local government, increasing numbers of public sector jobs lead to other challenges. Along with not-for-profit organisations such as charities and non-government organisations (NGOs), the public sector is the fastest growing area for finance jobs.

As commercial practices are put into effect in organisations as part of public sector reform, and the Public Finance Initiative, public sector accountants and finance specialists are in more demand.

There has never been such a crossover between industry and public sector. There are now aspects of the NHS run on commercial lines. Areas like risk management and resource management, used in commerce and industry, are being brought into the public sector.
Robert Jelly, Director of Education, CIMA

Accountancy Practice Hierarchy

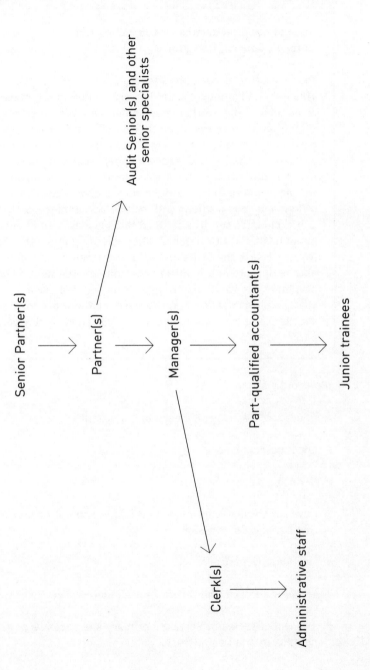

Head of financial services – £38,349–£43,059
Borough Council, Derbyshire
Salary scale: E12
Plus casual user car allowance
This outstanding opportunity has arisen due to the recent
promotion of the previous postholder. Following a critical
Audit Commission report on the council's corporate
governance arrangements we are looking for someone with
a balance of skills, knowledge and experience to make a
major contribution to our improvement plan. The postholder
will be required to act as the council's deputy Section 151
officer and your portfolio will include accountancy, audit
and exchequer services (council tax, payments and housing
benefits). A full CCAB qualification is essential for this post.
If you possess the skills and experience required and are
able to operate in a multi-dimensional environment as part
of a team, we would like to hear from you. We are a
changing organisation that is determined to move towards
excellence in local government – do you want to play your
part?

You could work in:

- Education – schools, colleges and universities

- Local government

- Central government

- Government agencies, such as the Environment Agency and the
  Countryside Commission

- The Audit Commission

- Law – the Police, the Crown Prosecution Service, courts

- The National Health Service – primary and secondary
  healthcare and health trusts

- Non-government organisations, such as Amnesty International and Greenpeace

- Charities.

Scottish National Heritage runs lots of unusual projects – like reintroducing the beaver to Scotland. We've also completed consultations over National Parks and access to the countryside. I manage a team of 20 and provide financial advice to help the organisation do as much as possible with its resources.

Andrew Lyell, Head of Finance for
Scottish National Heritage*

*Courtesy of CIPFA

Advantages of the public sector and not-for-profit organisations include:

- The challenge of working in a changing business environment

- Local availability of jobs, e.g. local government and education

- The security of being part of the 'establishment', e.g. Civil Service

- Less likelihood of long working hours and a lot of business travel than in practice, industry or commerce

- The opportunity to train and develop within a common structure

- The opportunity to learn transferable skills (e.g risk management) or to become a specialist in public sector issues (e.g. Value For Money), making job transfer within the sector easier

- The satisfaction of working for the common good and for causes close to your heart, e.g. charities and NGOs.

Finance Manager (Technical), Housing Association
Location   Based at St Neots, Shipley or Chippenham
Salary and benefits   c£28,000 p.a. plus Benefits including Pension & Flexi-time
Duration   Permanent
Skills Keeping our finances in shape is essential to the welfare of our residents. To ensure they reside in safe, comfortable and secure accommodation, we now need a Qualified Accountant to assist in a wide range of accounting functions. Reporting to the Financial Operations Director, your role will involve providing taxation advice, preparing quarterly VAT returns and finding ways to improve and develop the existing financial systems. You will also assist in the completion of statutory returns, update and maintain the Financial Procedure Manual and manage two members of staff. Excellent presentation skills are required along with extensive knowledge of computerised accounting systems, VAT and other taxation legislation. Experience of using Excel or a similar spreadsheet application is also essential, together with a full driving licence and a willingness to occasionally undertake overnight stays away from home.

Disadvantages of the public sector and not-for-profit organisations include:

- Pay disparity with industry and commerce. The salary difference is reducing, with more people moving from industry to the public sector: business skills need to be paid for. However, expect to earn up to 20% less than your counterpart in industry and much less than an accountant in the City. In addition, you probably won't be able to negotiate your own salary package as it will be part of a nationwide points system.

- The rigidity of working within the Civil Service or for a small part of a very large organisation, e.g. the NHS. If you enjoy informal working environments, think again. Your job may be prescribed and formal. Bureaucracy may be off-putting. Think about producing reports on everything – in triplicate!

- If you train in the public sector and specialise in public sector skills you are pretty much stuck in the public sector.

- Because of the issues involved in charity jobs, this area can present its own unique pressures.

Salary comparisons at Senior level (*Accountancy Age*/Comshare)

Business Sector	Public Sector	Public Practice
Ken Hydon, 58	Andrew Foster, 58	Mike Rake, 55
Financial Director, Vodaphone Group Appointed to board 1985	Controller, Audit Commission Appointed 1993, stands down 2003	Chairman, KPMG International, UK Senior Partner Appointed Chairman in 2002, UK Senior Partner since 1998
£1,327,000	£200,000	£1,600,000

INDUSTRY

Industry is the area going through the most changes on the financial front as the effects of international demands and trends are felt on the factory floor. Part of a finance employee's job is to predict how a company will be affected by legislation, the world economy, supply and demand and the money market. This can make for an exciting, if hair-raising job – if the accountant is allowed to do it.

Look at corporate information at Companies House and you'll see an accountant somewhere on the top team. If he (and it usually is a he) is not the Chief Executive, then he's Deputy CEO, Managing Director or Finance Director at the very least. Increasingly, accountants are elbowing their way into other functions at senior level. It is not unusual to see a qualified accountant as Head of Operations, Purchasing and Supply, or even Sales and Marketing.

Accountants have to keep up with changes in business, that's their job. The best accountants in industry are becoming more imaginative and creative. The best companies are allowing them to be.

Damian Wild, *Editor*, Accountancy Age

Those at the collecting, collating and checking information end of the scale have opportunities to climb the ladder too; you don't have to have magical initials after your name to succeed in industry. Specialist sector information and experience are prized, and any specific skills gained with one company will make you marketable to another. You may not have the authority to externally audit company accounts, but you may have the knowledge and expertise to conduct an effective internal audit.

Finance Manager
Location   Northampton
Salary and benefits   to £35k + benefits
Skills Working within the European Finance Operations Group, this Finance Manager will manage the consolidation, planning, forecasting and reporting of European Manufacturing overhead and variations, and deputise for the Head of European Finance Operations. Submission of consolidations to Head Office in line with timetables. Interpretation of results. Management and development of small team. Effective communication and management of financial consolidation processes across European Manufacturing locations.
Other details Refinement and improvement of processes and controls, on an ongoing basis. Ad hoc work as directed by Head/Director of European Financial Operations. Working and communicating effectively within the European Supply Chain organisation. Some European travel involved. The ideal candidate will be a CIMA Passed Finalist or with two years' post-qualification experience. Systems experience that would be beneficial: Hyperion, AS 400, CODA.

The one great advantage of accountancy is that money magicians are needed in companies whether they are doing well or badly. It may be mergers and acquisitions one year, corporate recovery the next. Accountancy practices predict market changes and offer services accordingly, but the people they work closely with are those within a company who have the knowledge and figures at their fingertips.

Advantages of working in industry:

- Many varied opportunities in a variety of sectors

- Opportunity to acquire highly transferable skills and knowledge and to use them internationally

- A grounding in accountancy that provides a core experience to take elsewhere, for instance, public sector, banking, entrepreneurship

- Opportunity for senior management and board positions overseeing functions other than finance and more general areas of company business

- Good employer support for learning and advancement

- Exciting and creative projects as the corporate environment changes due to international legislation and economics.

Disadvantages of working in industry:

- Some companies are stuck in a time warp and accountants are put in a box. It may be difficult to be creative and generalist in some organisations

- A lot of dreary accounting work to be done on the way up

- Less job security than in recent times as worldwide recession takes a hold on the UK

- Primarily male-orientated at senior and boardroom level

● The increasing need (and expectation) to move around to gain relevant experience and the chance for promotion. OK if you're young, free and single.

I really enjoy my job as Finance Manager of Operations. It involves looking after the profit and loss account. The contribution provided by Operations is weighed up against the costs incurred by the company. I appraise the cost of fixed assets and investments, manufacturing and logistics, and creditors and inventory. It's busy and challenging; and it's fun!

Susannah Hamilton, Finance Manager, European Engineering Company, England

---

Revenue Analyst
Location   Leatherhead, Surrey
Salary and benefits   £30–32K
Duration   Permanent
Job description Assist with the management accounts and month end process for all revenue streams and related costs. Assistance with delivery of daily, weekly and monthly revenue reporting requirements. Assistance with streamlining current procedures.
Preparation of daily, weekly and monthly management accounts for all revenue streams and related costs including preparation of accruals, prepayments and deferrals. Reconciliation of related balance sheet control accounts. Assistance with revenue reporting requirements including design and preparation of daily, weekly and monthly management and shareholder report. In-depth analysis of revenue and related costs including preparation and interpretation of key performance indicators, variance and trend analysis. Assistance with streamlining current process/procedures by review of current process and

recommendations for changes to speed monthly reporting
timescales.
Other details Involvement with further source systems
development to ensure end-to-end integrated revenue
recognition solution for all revenue streams. Assistance in
maintenance of systems, i.e. report generators and chart of
accounts structure. Assistance in preparation of short- and
long-term forecasts for input to budgets and business plans.
Operational experience: minimum of two years' all round
accounting experience (IT telecom preferred); revenue
analyst experience. Personal characteristics: highly
analytical; ability to work under pressure; ability to meet
deadlines; team player; sound commercial acumen.
Intermediate/finalist stage CIMA or equivalent.

BANKING AND THE CITY

Commerce, as it is generally known, includes banks (high
street, corporate and investment), insurance companies,
stockbroker firms, venture capitalists and any other
organisations in the financial services sector. These days the
lines between each of the above are more blurred than ever,
with companies frequently offering a range of financial services.
Accountancy firms (see Accountancy Practice, above) are
treading on the toes of investment banks, increasingly
competing for similar projects.

Probably the largest growing area in this sector is insurance as
more products become available (such as private healthcare),
competition is fierce, and the market changes. Other areas of
commerce are not so positive. General consumer banking has
contracted due to takeovers and the internationalisation of the
industry, with four or five core organisations running the show.
Investment banking, like stockbroking, offers fewer
opportunities than it did in the buoyant 1990s as money
markets decline and economic growth slows. But it's not all
bad news.

An Example of the Corporate Financial Hierarchy for an Industrial Company

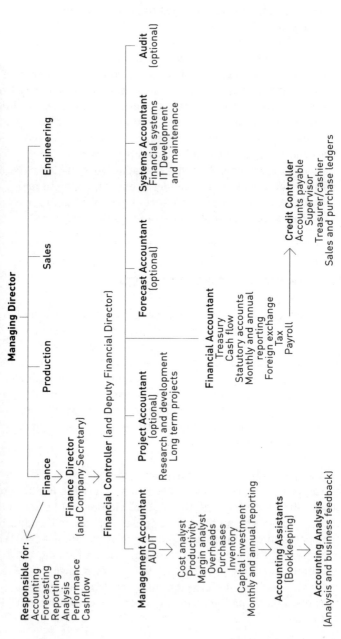

Managing Director

Responsible for:
Accounting
Forecasting
Reporting
Analysis
Performance
Cashflow

Finance — Production — Sales — Engineering

Finance Director
(and Company Secretary)

Financial Controller (and Deputy Financial Director)

Management Accountant
AUDIT

Cost analyst
Productivity
Margin analyst
Overheads
Purchases
Inventory
Capital investment
Monthly and annual reporting

Accounting Assistants
(Bookkeeping)

Accounting Analysis
(Analysis and business feedback)

Project Accountant
(optional)
Research and development
Long term projects

Financial Accountant
Treasury
Cash flow
Statutory accounts
Monthly and annual reporting
Foreign exchange
Tax
Payroll

Credit Controller
Accounts payable
Supervisor
Treasurer/cashier
Sales and purchase ledgers

Forecast Accountant
(optional)

Systems Accountant
Financial systems
IT Development
and maintenance

Audit
(optional)

The City (of London) has long been well known as the place to find a high-powered, fast-paced, ridiculously well-paid job, and like all industries, banking needs accountants to function. These days the City lacks the pace and confidence of the past decade, but still provides opportunities for those with an excellent academic record and first-rate interpersonal skills.

Generally there are two areas of accountancy: client-facing (including equity analysis, fund management, corporate finance and private equity); and business support (including a variety of finance roles and risk management). Every organisation has to have accountants for audit, assurance and tax management, as well as corporate development. As well as internal services in support of a financial institution, its customers also want financial and business advice.

In the rapidly changing marketplace, you have to be able to extract and interpret critical pieces of information quickly. Training as a Chartered Accountant has equipped me for this task.
Jemma Houlihan, Senior Equity Analyst, ABN AMRO Stockbrokers*

*Courtesy of ICAI

Many high-fliers in the City have entered the sector without formal finance or business qualifications but have applied a good brain, a lot of confidence and a tremendous amount of high-stress hours to gaining the right kind of experience. In the City those who get on can get to the top fast, while those who can't take the pace burn out at a young age.

The risks are not so high for qualified accountants entering the City, although it is common for employees to move from job to job in rapid succession. Although job insecurity and intense pressure are the downsides to a job in the City, it's still the best paid work available for accountants in this country.

Finance Manager, Insurance
Location   Letchworth, Hertfordshire
Salary and benefits   GBP 45–50,000 plus PMI, pension, PHI
and life assurance after qualifying period
Duration   Permanent
Skills A qualified accountant (ACA, CIMA, ACCA – minimum
2–3 years) with an insurance sector background, you will also
need experience of completing FSA Returns and Corporation
Tax Returns. This role demands a high degree of IT expertise
with the ability to produce effective and accurate verbal,
numerical and written communications for all levels.
Other details   We want to be the best private medical
insurer in the market and you can help us get there. This
role, reporting directly to the Chief Executive Officer, is vital
to ensure the preparation of statutory accounts and budgets,
the completion of regulatory returns, effective handling of
investments and treasury and the supply of extensive and
timely management information to the business.

Advantages of banking and the City:

- Good money and employee benefits

- Fast-track opportunities (in the City) to gain seniority at a
relatively young age

- Opportunity to gain specialist financial services sector
knowledge and experience which is transferable between a
variety of institutions

- Exciting and exacting projects to work on as the financial
sector experiences ongoing changes

- Opportunities for women.

*Approaching the end of my second year, I have
worked in Group Finance, Standard Life bank and
the property, treasury and private equity*

departments of Standard Life Investments. I have been involved in producing an annual report and accounts, the bank's quarterly statutory returns to the Bank of England, and competitor analysis of investment returns in private equity funds. My experience is constantly changing and I have been kept on a steep learning curve.

Pauline Campbell, Trainee Accountant,
Standard Life Assurance Company*

*Courtesy of ICAS

Disadvantages of banking and the City:

- Lack of security in some City institutions as market conditions change swiftly

- High-paced, highly-pressurised work in some areas

- Some City jobs are ageist

- Decreasing number of opportunities

- Highly competitive to enter

- Some financial institutions may seem exciting but there may be a lot of routine work that leaves little time for creative projects

- A lot of red tape as the financial sector is regulation bound.

Qualified Accountants – Business Unit Control

Company:	**Investment Bank**
Remuneration:	**£Competitive**
Location:	**UK – London**
Position type:	**Permanent**

These roles lie within our Business Unit Control (BUC) function, which is responsible for providing appropriate levels of operational and analytical support to assist Senior Managers in their business decisions. BUCs measure and manage actual performance against strategic plans and provide the analysis and reporting of revenues as well as the direct and allocated business costs.

Minimum Job Requirements:
* Educated to degree level (2.1 minimum)
* Either CIMA or ACA first time passes
* 2–5 years' post-qualification experience (preferably in investment banking)
* MIS experience
* Displays accuracy and attention to detail at all times
* Product knowledge
* Good communication skills
* Team player
* Ability to deliver under pressure and display ideas, energy, drive and commitment

For all the advantages and disadvantages of working in different areas, the real conclusion (just as the institutes say) is that a professional qualification in accountancy is a passport to almost any business or industry, almost anywhere in the world.

DID YOU KNOW?
The average student starting salary for 2001 was £13,787. (ICAS)

CHAPTER 4

Case studies

Finding out the facts is a good start for anyone interested in the profession as a future career, but for the real take on the pros and cons of life as an accountant, you can't beat first-hand knowledge.

This chapter is devoted to six short case studies of accountants in a variety of work and from different backgrounds. There are the views and backgrounds of a young woman who came to practice accountancy after having a child, the high-powered financial manager in a European engineering company, the Big Four graduate, the practice trainee who swapped a life in farming for accountancy practice, the accountant who works in an international NGO and who took a pay cut to get there, and the accounting technician who has combined working for the family firm with offering a freelance bookkeeping service from home.

We haven't covered every accountancy experience in this chapter, and the case studies do not represent every job or every course on offer, but we'd like to give you a chance to hear how it is for some who have followed different career paths.

Most important of all, these interviews, along with the quotes that appear throughout the book, portray a personal picture of the reality of accountancy today.

Amanda Knight

Amanda Knight is Audit Senior at the small practice of Richard Mainwaring in Hereford. She has worked at the firm for two years and qualified as a Certified Accountant (ACCA) in 2002. Amanda enjoys practice work and was pleased to complete her ACCA after studying for seven years.

'While at school I wanted to work in finance and was pushed towards banking. However, after studying for a BTEC National Certificate in Business and Finance I really enjoyed the accountancy part of the syllabus and wanted to pursue it further.

'I was able to study with a BTEC (which is equal to an A-level) and I could complete the required three years on-the-job training either before, during or after taking the exams. That suited me because when I left college I was expecting my daughter and wanted to combine a career with motherhood.

'I started the ACCA in 1995 and completed the first stage in two years. The second part took just a year, and then I took a two-year break because of job changes. From the point of practising, there is no difference to the more traditional qualifications (ACA and CA) and I have the same entitlements. There is a difference however, in the training and exam structure. I chose the ACCA route because it is more flexible – I wanted study to fit in with family life – and I wasn't a graduate.

'I am lucky because my employers were enthusiastic about me finishing my exams. They have been actively supportive by granting me study leave, paying for my training and giving me paid time off to attend exams. Some practices aren't so flexible.

'In larger practices accountants can specialise, but I prefer working in a small practice. It's satisfying being able to provide a range of services, from accounts preparation and auditing, to tax advice.

'Many people don't realise what a "people" job accountancy is. It's important to gain respect and establish a good long-term relationship with a client. I have to know the detail of their businesses, and consequently, I get an insight into people's worlds.

'I am happy to stay where I am for the next two to five years. I'd like to develop my career within the practice and to see what evolves. Accountancy is a profession which changes regularly – there is always new law to learn and new accountancy measures.

'I am sure the role is changing for women too. When I was a trainee there were many more women than men studying. Accountancy is a good career for women. It's an industry that is becoming more flexible. There are roles for part-time workers and getting qualified is now easier than ever to fit in with working and domestic life.'

Ben Joseph
Ben Joseph, 23, is training for the ACA qualification at global professional services firm, Ernst & Young. He studied History at University College London and organised a summer internship at E&Y in his second year. This gave him a tempting taste of the accountancy life in a large firm, which encouraged Ben to apply for training at all of the Big Five firms. Ernst & Young invited him back and he completed his first year as an Associate in the Audit Division in September 2003.

'For the first three months I went to college to learn basic technical skills, then from December I became involved in client-facing work for the division. It may seem scary but because the culture of E&Y is so geared to graduate training, both the firm and the client are aware of the relationship and it works well. Most of the time I deal with people at the same level as me, so we all learn from one another. It's a prerequisite of the qualification that I have a minimum of three years' work experience.

'I'm really happy here and know I chose the right career path. There are so many advantages to getting a chartered qualification in accountancy, but probably the most obvious one is the doors it opens. Those letters after your name are internationally respected and the training can form the basis for many different jobs. Everyone knows what you've done to get there.

'The other big advantage is security – that's why there's been such an increase in qualified accountants in recent years. In a market that's changeable it's good to know you've got a professional qualification behind you. It impresses girlfriends' parents anyway, as they know you'll always be employed!

'I chose accountancy because I was interested in business, but I wasn't sure which area of business I wanted to specialise in. Accountancy is perfect because it gives me good technical skills and knowledge as well as the chance to see many sides of business. So far I've been taken by corporate finance and investment banking, but I'd also like to travel around the world working on small projects, or I could become an entrepreneur – who knows?

'What's impressed me most is the emphasis on teamwork. Everything we do is based on an interactive team structure. That's good grounding for any profession but it particularly applies to accounts; you have to be able to work across many different functions. My experience at E&Y certainly dispels the image of an accountant counting beans in a dusty corner. It is not a solitary job at all. Here there's no escape from the crowd; we don't even have our own desks to hide at!

'That's what's good about accountancy; it provides you with so many useful tools. I hope to make good use of them.'

Douglas Brewster

Douglas Brewster is a Financial Accountant for an international non-government organisation based in London. He is 56 years old and has worked in accountancy since graduating with a Maths Honours degree from the University of St Andrews. Previously an industry accountant, he has been working for an NGO for the last 17 years.

'I started life in finance in a Cost Office, and immediately started a CIMA qualification. After gaining experience with two companies, I moved back to Scotland to work for Metal Box.

'At Metal Box I spent 13 years moving around learning about different processes. Access to and understanding of the shop floor is important, it puts your work into context.

'At the factory I was responsible for accounting on a monthly basis. It was my job to provide accounts to go to head office. Within the Accounts Department I was operating petty cash and payroll, as well as the factory bank account, detailing invoices and sales payments.

'I learnt what was behind the figures, then got into management roles. The higher up the ladder you go the more generalist your work becomes. The emphasis is taken off the detail and having a business overview becomes important. It's less dealing with figures, more dealing with people.

'I finally settled at Group and Overseas Head Office. There I was consolidating results from the various companies and feeding data on to an IBM. It was cutting edge technology at that time!

'The job at the NGO in London came up when I was living in Reading and wanting to stay there. I had to take a drop in salary – which is usual when going from industry to a not-for-profit organisation. People literally do it for love. I wanted to use my accounting skills for a good cause.

'The big difference in working for an NGO is that people are here – in whatever function – because they really want to be. Many come because they have a burning interest in an issue, some because they have their own agenda.

'Working for a non-profit-making organisation is just like any other, but the emphasis is different. Production is not so tangible. Here, the product is education and information rather than a tin can; it makes it difficult to evaluate performance.

'I was head of the Accounts Department for five years but I found managing people difficult. I then moved to a Project Accountant role and felt happier. It has some aspects of management combined with the technical side.

'It's amazing how many people are interested in working for charities and NGOs. I think people want more out of life and their jobs than a pay packet. My advice is not to be starry-eyed. It is special, but it's not that special. You can be an idealist, but don't expect the working environment to be ideal. In fact, it may be a more difficult place to work than most, because there are so many idealists.'

Julie Pullen

Julie Pullen is 34 and in her final year of study for the AAT (Associate Accounting Technician) qualification. She has worked as office manager for the family company for the last ten years, as well as taking part-time jobs in bookkeeping roles. Now she has successfully completed two years of the AAT, she is setting up as a self-employed bookkeeper for small local businesses. Julie's ambition is to become a fully qualified Chartered Accountant via the ICAEW fast track scheme.

'Although I had been doing the books, operating payroll, VAT returns and profit and loss accounts for my husband's company, Tree Management, for five years, I felt I wanted an exam in accounts. Also, I thought it would help the business in the long run by cutting accountants' costs!

'Although I knew the basics from practical experience and had the option to skip the first year AAT Foundation stage, I thought it would be good for me to gain some knowledge – as well as some confidence – by starting at the beginning. I'm pleased I did because those students I met who went straight into the second year struggled.

'It's not just the content of the course, but the learning curve too. Going back into education can be hard. The Foundation is only one exam so it eases you back into studying.

'I've always enjoyed numbers, but my interest really came through the business. It fascinates me how you can start a business from nothing and build it. I love to balance. My husband deals with the management, technical and client-facing side of the business and I do the rest. We're quite compatible, as I like to stay in the background. But I'm the one who gives the go-ahead on capital spend or employing more staff. I have control of the money, therefore I have the power!

'At school I enjoyed maths and in particular, RSA Bookkeeping, but I didn't pursue it. I wanted to work and earn money. In the office jobs I had after school, I ended up entering sales or purchase ledgers because it came naturally to me. Working with numbers is a bit like Marmite, it's something you either love or hate.

'I think anyone wanting to study accountancy part-time has to have a genuine interest in it. Discipline and dedication help too. It's not easy taking professional courses when you've a business, a home and a family to look after.

'Every Sunday morning I dedicated three hours to going back over the week's lesson to ensure I understood it. I crammed for the exam by getting up at 5am each day revising lessons and practising past papers. As a result, I found the exam straightforward.

'Confidence, problem-solving skills and multi-tasking are all important in bookkeeping but there's no getting away from the fact that you have to be mathematically-minded.'

Susannah Hamilton

Susannah works for a large European engineering company in England at senior management level, as Finance Manager for Operations. She attained a professional qualification from CIMA (Certified Institute of Management Accounting) six years ago and has worked for the same organisation for the last 15 years. She is now looking for a new challenge.

'At 18 I had originally wanted to study English and Drama at university but changed my mind in favour of on-the-job training. On leaving school I got a job as a Commercial Accounts Trainee at a manufacturing company and began a two-year Institute of Export course that was finance-based. My main job at that time was cash collection and credit control.

'As I got two As and a B at A-level, I was offered a place at Manchester University to do Accounting with Economics and Finance. It appealed to me but I was offered a promotion and pay increase with the manufacturing company and that convinced me to stay!

'After five years there and a short time in a marketing office, I moved to the engineering company's finance department as Sales

Accounting Manager, recognising that corporate finance within manufacturing was what I really wanted to do.

'I started in charge of a team of 14 in cash controlling, but I had only really covered sales and purchase ledger. As the company restructured I took the opportunity to study for the Certificate of Management Studies, which I did from a home correspondence course.

'As I achieved four As in my first CIMA exams, first time, I began to get noticed in the finance department. Although I had been a manager at the company, it was only my success in gaining the professional qualification that put me in the running for promotion. I was asked to cover maternity leave within Management Accounting and have continued to work my way up since then.

'In the last four years the company has been examining lean manufacturing and is attempting to create a lean enterprise. This has real implications for accounting. Following these developments as well as keeping up within accounts is challenging and interesting.

'You need to like working with people as 90% of the accountant's job is communication. Interacting at all levels of the company, as well as externally, is a rewarding dimension of the job.

'I am rarely at my desk and catch up on paperwork after office hours. I have regular meetings with employees from all sections of the company and that's how most of my day is taken up. Communication is very important. I need to get the correct information from people but also help them understand what is important and why. That can be difficult as there is frequently a fear of finance – accountants can be seen as controllers, or the policemen of the company.'

Tim Brown

Tim Brown is 30 years old and completes his ACCA qualification in December 2003. He came to accountancy as a mature student at 27, having originally studied agriculture. He works for Burton Sweet, an accountancy practice with five offices in South-West England.

'I was originally running the family farm, milking 120 cows a day, but I had to stop work when I broke my leg playing rugby. I got to know the accountant because I was doing the bookkeeping and I asked him if there were any opportunities. Farming had become very difficult and I was looking for more security.

'My boss had a good instinct about me and pushed me straight into the AAT (Associate of Accounting Technicians) Intermediate level and I passed all the exams first time. After that, he suggested I went for the ACCA (Associate Chartered Certified Accountant) qualification to become an accountant.

'In some ways I wish I had started earlier as I've taken to it naturally. I really enjoy the variety of work and the different businesses. I deal with a variety of tradesmen and I've brought in my own clients.

'The client relationship is very important. I get a buzz out of helping people and I find the job very satisfying. I can turn incomplete records into a set of accounts. I can understand scribbles because I've been used to it at the farm! The detective work is what I really like. Often I can have a bigger degree of confidence when someone comes in with a plastic bag of receipts. You then have to load accounts from bank statements.

'It's gone really well and I have enjoyed it. I am glad I came to it older as it's a slog; working on a farm got me used to hard work! It takes discipline to study and it's not always easy. I had a son in January 2003, which makes life more difficult, but I'm lucky I have a very understanding wife!

'I am a careerist accountant and I'd like to stay with Burton Sweet for the foreseeable future. They have been very supportive throughout my training and are encouraging about future opportunities.

'I don't think accountancy is for everyone, but if you can get focused, like talking to people and find business interesting, it can be very rewarding.'

CHAPTER 5

Is Accountancy for me?

The first four chapters of this book have been an introduction to accountancy. If you're still interested in accounting as a career, read on to see if you've got what it takes.

EXPECTATIONS QUIZ

What do you expect life would be like as an accountant?

Tick the statements you think are true.

1. Accountants must be happy working on a computer all day

2. Accountants must have an eye for detail

3. Accountants must be good at maths

4. Accountants need a basic understanding of general software packages

5. Accountants need to be happy working on their own

6. Accountants must have good written and oral communication skills

7. Accountants have to know about business

8. Accountants are boring!

9. Accountants need to have analytical minds

10. Accountants must work on their own initiative

11. Accountants must be academic.

Answers on page 61.

I want a career path that offers different possibilities – it suits my personality. Accountancy also suits me because I have an interest in numbers, an analytical mind and a fundamental interest in business.

Ben Joseph, Trainee Accountant,
Ernst & Young, London

PERSONAL SUITABILITY CHECKLIST

Have you got what it takes to be an accountant?

There are no right or wrong answers; someone working in an area of accountancy could have uttered all the statements below. Tick the statements that sound most like you. Read on and refer to the Expectations Quiz answers for further information.

1. I am fascinated by business and commerce

2. I really enjoy working with colleagues as part of a team

3.   I am a natural with numbers

4.   I can easily stand back and look at the big picture

5.   I am a creative problem solver

6.   I am ambitious and competitive

7.   I enjoy academic study, research and analysis

8.   I am good at influencing people

9.   I like being part of a formal structure

10.   I have good IT skills and enjoy working with different systems

11.   I have good judgement

12.   I enjoy managing projects

13.   I am happy providing a service to clients

14.   I enjoy going out and getting new business

15.   I am a confident communicator

16.   I am flexible and versatile

17.   I want to run a business in the future

18.   I like finding out how organisations tick

19.   I am organised and multi-tasking

20.   I'd like to work abroad.

There is a degree of consistency of qualities and skills in this practice. Everyone has to know their stuff – that's the technical competence required – in addition, people need an understanding of business and risk management, the ability to work effectively within a team, balanced with a strong sense of the individual, and good problem-solving ability.

Stevan Rolls, Director of Resourcing and Employee Integration, Ernst & Young

---

EXPECTATIONS QUIZ – ANSWERS

1. **Accountants must be happy working on a computer all day**
   As a bookkeeper or trainee audit accountant you may expect to spend a substantial amount of time on the computer, but it's a general equation that the more you progress up the career ladder, the less computer-based work you'll have to do. Senior posts become less technical, less detailed, and more customer-facing, with a decrease in desk work.

2. **Accountants must have an eye for detail**
   Attention to detail is a requirement of most jobs these days and when trends have to be analysed and figures need to be read, you need to be able to spot errors quickly. Accountants generally deal with a lot of detail, especially in audit, accounts and tax areas, so patience is a virtue too!

3. **Accountants must be good at maths**
   Excellent maths ability used to be a key skill as all figures work was done manually. Nowadays, however, computer programs take care of the numbers and maths is no longer a large part of an accountant's job. Most importantly, accountants need to be able to see what's behind the figures, and a recognition of numbers remains a useful accounting skill.

It's important to have a head for figures, but it's not the most important thing. Software takes care of a lot of the calculation. What's most important is what's behind the figures. You have to know when the figures look right. Having an inquisitive mind is a good thing.

Tim Brown, Trainee Accountant, Burton Sweet, Bristol

4. **Accountants need a basic understanding of general software packages**
    IT skills are essential for accountants as the emphasis moves from number-crunching to number and fact analysis via computers. There are many financial software systems in use, from payroll to procurement, and an accountant needs to be proficient in the use of (and sometimes implementation of) software relevant to his or her area of expertise. Increasingly, employees in the finance function of organisations, as well as in practice, are managing IT systems and departments. A talent for IT is a very useful transferable skill.

5. **Accountants need to be happy working on their own**
    Accounting is a 'people job' and there will be very few roles where an accountant is able to hide in a corner of an office all day. Bookkeeping may be a more solitary job, but accountants have to be able to work in multi-functional teams, liaise effectively with clients and manage their own departments. Accountants must have good people skills and enjoy working with people at all levels in an organisation.

One of the most important requirements is people skills. The old stereotype of an accountant as an introverted bookworm forming relationships with numbers, not people, is gone. This business is all about dealing with people. For instance, the audit is an objective, data-driven process. But how you engage with people in the client company while collecting and analysing audit information is very important. There are very few circumstances where people are working entirely on their own.

Stevan Rolls, Director of Resourcing and Employee Integration, Ernst & Young

6. **Accountants must have good written and oral communcation skills**
   Working in finance involves negotiating, influencing, promoting and advising and that means communication skills – both spoken and written – are paramount. Writing reports, giving presentations and consulting with colleagues are part of an accountant's daily job, so if these are not your strengths, think again.

You've got to bring a lot of people skills to the job – I never realised that. There are some in accountancy who will never progress far because they just can't communicate well enough.

Tim Brown, Trainee Accountant, Burton Sweet, Bristol

7. **Accountants have to know about business**
   Most importantly, if you think you'd like a career in accounting, you must have a fundamental interest in business. Whichever branch you work in – practice, industry, commerce or not-for-profit – a fascination for

the internal and external workings of business is essential. Keeping up with business trends, legislation, the economy, the Stock Exchange and the FTSE 100 are an important part of an accountant's job.

8. **Accountants are boring!**
Some accountants are! However, the stereotype of a boring accountant is rapidly changing and increasingly accountants are becoming the influential dynamic and creative force in many organisations.

We work in a fast-moving marketplace that covers the world, so we need dynamic, well-trained finance people who can keep up.

Steve Taylor, Vice President,
Paramount Pictures, USA*

*Courtesy of ACCA

9. **Accountants need to have analytical minds**
Analysis of research, figures, facts, trends and strategy is important in an accountant's job. Having a mind that naturally orders information and sees past the obvious is a useful talent. Having an investigative urge or being naturally inquisitive is helpful too!

10. **Accountants must work on their own initiative**
Accountants do have to be able to trust their own judgement and make high-level decisions based on technical knowledge and expertise. However, accountants have to work as part of a team and colleagues from other disciplines or functions need to have input, so an accountant will make decisions based on discussion. Importantly, initiative is not always enough when decisions have to be checked against legislation, ethical codes, regulation and restriction – accountants cannot afford to be rogue workers.

11. **Accountants must be academic**
    Accountants with professional qualifications from one of
    the six institutes do have to be able to undertake
    academic study continuing well past initial qualification.
    In order to earn a well-respected acronym, an
    accountant has to commit to continuing development
    through his or her career. There are more vocational,
    less academic routes into accountancy (see Chapter 7
    for further information), but many financial roles
    demand study, training, learning and exam-taking.

If you think a future in accountancy is for you, read on. If in doubt,
turn to Chapter 10 for alternative careers that may prove a better
fit.

CHAPTER 6

What is an accountant?

The term 'accountant' may be applied to anyone working in accountancy. Unlike 'architect', for instance, it's not limited to those with the professional qualification. In order to distinguish the qualified accountants with a recognised professional status (those allowed by law to audit company accounts) from others, we'll call them Professional Accountants.

All Professional Accountants have chartered status. This status is acquired after postgraduate-level professional training and on-the-job experience provided by four main accountancy institutes. See the diagram on the next page for an overview.

There is a second category of accountants at this postgraduate level, and within this guide we'll called them Specialised Accountants. Their qualifications are chartered and are at the same level as Professional Accountants, but they have chosen a particular slant on accountancy and have studied different subjects. Unlike Professional Accountants, this group is not allowed to audit company accounts.

Chartered and Certified – The Qualifications For Professional Accountancy in the UK

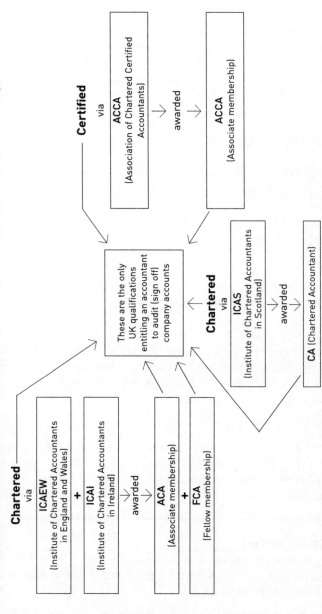

Chartered

via

ICAEW
(Institute of Chartered Accountants in England and Wales)

+

ICAI
(Institute of Chartered Accountants in Ireland)

→ awarded →

ACA
(Associate membership)

+

FCA
(Fellow membership)

Certified

via

ACCA
(Association of Chartered Certified Accountants)

→ awarded →

ACCA
(Associate membership)

These are the only UK qualifications entitling an accountant to audit (sign off) company accounts

Chartered

via

ICAS
(Institute of Chartered Accountants in Scotland)

→ awarded →

CA (Chartered Accountant)

N.B. – unlike 'architect', 'accountant' is not a protected title and anyone working in accountancy can call themselves an accountant. However, the term 'professional accountant' has been adopted to distinguish those with the ACA/FCA and ACCA titles.

Professional Accountants have the letters ACA, CA or ACCA after their names, while Specialised Accountants adopt either CMA or CPFA.

Investigating accountancy qualifications is like entering a spaghetti junction of institute comparisons on training, exams, entry requirements, exemptions and acronyms. If you want to find out about becoming an accountant, become familiar with the acronyms, as there are many, and they are confusing. Look at the diagrams on pages 69–74.

CHARTERED ACCOUNTANTS

The ACA (Associate Chartered Accountant) is awarded by the biggest accounting body in Europe, the Institute of Chartered Accountants for England and Wales (ICAEW). This is the most popular qualification for graduate training in the largest UK accountancy firms.

The CA (Chartered Accountant) award is given by the oldest professional body of accountants in the world, the Institute of Chartered Accountants in Scotland (ICAS).

Like the ACA, the CA confers the status of chartered on its qualified members. Both of these are postgraduate qualifications and form the basis of graduate training at the Big Four – the most sought-after public practice positions for high-performing graduates from around the world.

The third and last of the Chartered Accountancy qualifications is the Irish ACA (Associate Chartered Accountant), awarded by the ICAI (the Institute of Chartered Accountants in Ireland). This body covers both Northern Ireland and the Republic of Ireland, and has offices in Belfast and Dublin.

DID YOU KNOW?
In seven of the top ten Irish financial services companies, Chartered Accountants hold the position of Chief Executive or Financial Director. (ICAI)

Postgraduate Level Qualifications in Accountancy (1)

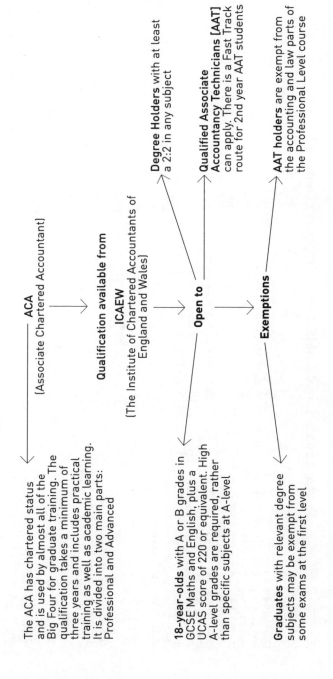

ACA
(Associate Chartered Accountant)

The ACA has chartered status and is used by almost all of the Big Four for graduate training. The qualification takes a minimum of three years and includes practical training as well as academic learning. It is divided into two main parts: Professional and Advanced

Qualification available from

ICAEW
(The Institute of Chartered Accountants of England and Wales)

Open to

Degree Holders with at least a 2:2 in any subject

Qualified Associate Accountancy Technicians [AAT] can apply. There is a Fast Track route for 2nd year AAT students

18-year-olds with A or B grades in GCSE Maths and English, plus a UCAS score of 220 or equivalent. High A-level grades are required, rather than specific subjects at A-level

Exemptions

AAT holders are exempt from the accounting and law parts of the Professional Level course

Graduates with relevant degree subjects may be exempt from some exams at the first level

Postgraduate Level Qualifications in Accountancy (2)

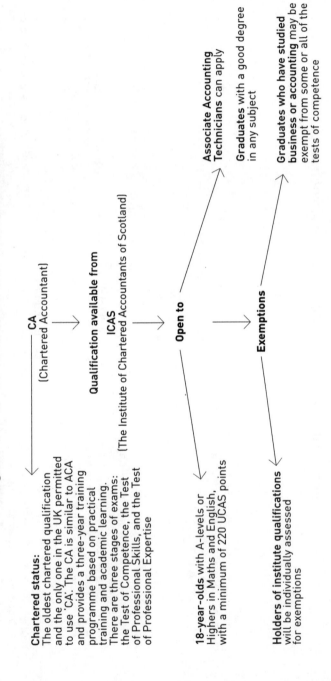

CA
(Chartered Accountant)

Chartered status:
The oldest chartered qualification and the only one in the UK permitted to use 'CA'. The CA is similar to ACA and provides a three-year training programme based on practical training and academic learning. There are three stages of exams: the Test of Competence, the Test of Professional Skills, and the Test of Professional Expertise

Qualification available from

ICAS
(The Institute of Chartered Accountants of Scotland)

Open to

18-year-olds with A-levels or Highers in Maths and English, with a minimum of 220 UCAS points

Exemptions

Holders of institute qualifications will be individually assessed for exemptions

Associate Accounting Technicians can apply

Graduates with a good degree in any subject

Graduates who have studied business or accounting may be exempt from some or all of the tests of competence

Postgraduate Level Qualifications in Accountancy (3)

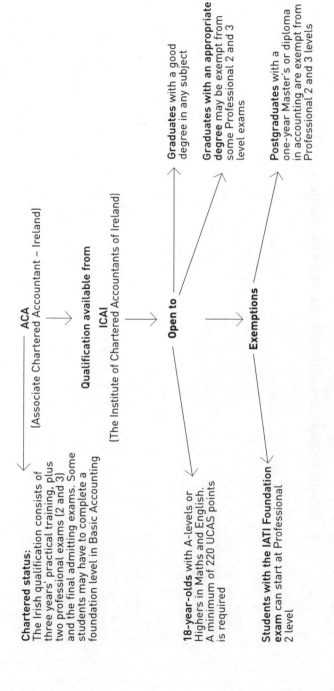

ACA
(Associate Chartered Accountant – Ireland)

Chartered status:
The Irish qualification consists of three years' practical training, plus two professional exams (2 and 3) and the final admitting exams. Some students may have to complete a foundation level in Basic Accounting

Qualification available from

ICAI
(The Institute of Chartered Accountants of Ireland)

Open to

Graduates with a good degree in any subject

18-year-olds with A-levels or Highers in Maths and English. A minimum of 220 UCAS points is required

Exemptions

Graduates with an appropriate degree may be exempt from some Professional 2 and 3 level exams

Students with the IATI Foundation exam can start at Professional 2 level

Postgraduates with a one-year Master's or diploma in accounting are exempt from Professional 2 and 3 levels

Postgraduate Level Qualifications in Accountancy (4)

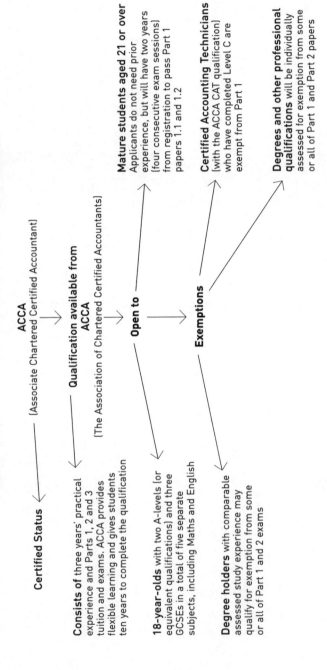

Certified Status →
(Associate Chartered Certified Accountant)

Qualification available from ACCA →
(The Association of Chartered Certified Accountants)

Consists of three years' practical experience and Parts 1, 2 and 3 tuition and exams. ACCA provides flexible learning and gives students ten years to complete the qualification

Open to

18-year-olds with two A-levels (or equivalent qualifications) and three GCSEs in a total of five separate subjects, including Maths and English

Mature students aged 21 or over
Applicants do not need prior experience, but will have two years (four consecutive exam sessions) from registration to pass Part 1 papers 1.1 and 1.2

Exemptions

Degree holders with comparable assessed study experience may qualify for exemption from some or all of Part 1 and 2 exams

Certified Accounting Technicians (with the ACCA CAT qualification) who have completed Level C are exempt from Part 1

Degrees and other professional qualifications will be individually assessed for exemption from some or all of Part 1 and Part 2 papers

Postgraduate Level Qualifications in Accountancy (5)

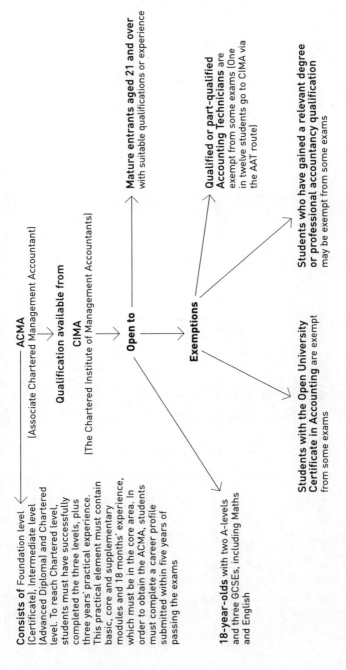

Consists of Foundation level (Certificate), Intermediate level (Advanced Diploma) and Chartered level. To reach Chartered level, students must have successfully completed the three levels, plus three years' practical experience. This practical element must contain basic, core and supplementary modules and 18 months' experience, which must be in the core area. In order to obtain the ACMA, students must complete a career profile submitted within five years of passing the exams

ACMA
(Associate Chartered Management Accountant)

Qualification available from

CIMA
(The Chartered Institute of Management Accountants)

Open to

Mature entrants aged 21 and over with suitable qualifications or experience

18-year-olds with two A-levels and three GCSEs, including Maths and English

Exemptions

Students with the Open University Certificate in Accounting are exempt from some exams

Qualified or part-qualified Accounting Technicians are exempt from some exams (One in twelve students go to CIMA via the AAT route)

Students who have gained a relevant degree or professional accountancy qualification may be exempt from some exams

Postgraduate Level Qualifications in Accountancy (6)

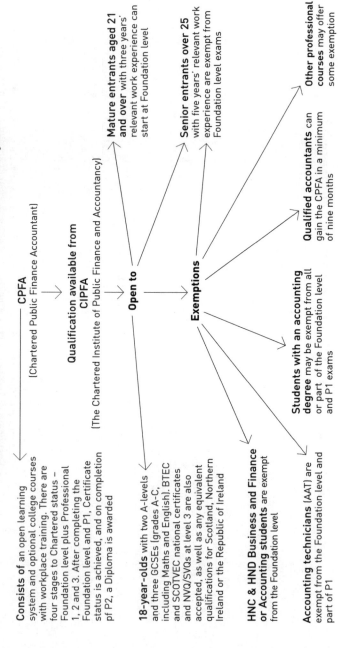

CPFA
(Chartered Public Finance Accountant)

Qualification available from CIPFA
(The Chartered Institute of Public Finance and Accountancy)

Consists of an open learning system and optional college courses with workplace training. There are four stages to Chartered status – Foundation level plus Professional 1, 2 and 3. After completing the Foundation level and P1, Certificate status is achieved, and on completion pf P2, a Diploma is awarded

Open to

Mature entrants aged 21 and over with three years' relevant work experience can start at Foundation level

Senior entrants over 25 with five years' relevant work experience are exempt from Foundation level exams

Exemptions

Other professional courses may offer some exemption

Qualified accountants can gain the CPFA in a minimum of nine months

Students with an accounting degree may be exempt from all or part of the Foundation level and P1 exams

HNC & HND Business and Finance or Accounting students are exempt from the Foundation level

Accounting technicians (AAT) are exempt from the Foundation level and part of P1

18-year-olds with two A-levels and three GCSEs (grades A–C, including Maths and English). BTEC and SCOTVEC national certificates and NVQ/SVQs at level 3 are also accepted, as well as any equivalent qualifications for Scotland, Northern Ireland or the Republic of Ireland

Recognition of these three institutes is equal and their qualifications open doors in business and finance around the world. One of the many advantages of successfully completing professional accountancy training is the outstanding reputation of the institutes and the high-quality training they provide.

CHARTERED CERTIFIED ACCOUNTANTS

Relatively new to chartered status, and in the past best known for certified status, is the ACCA (Associate Chartered Certified Accountant) from the body with the same acronym, ACCA (Association of Chartered Certificated Accountants).

DID YOU KNOW?
ACCA is the largest and fastest-growing international accountancy body, with over 300,000 students and members in 160 countries. ACCA has 70 staffed offices and other centres around the world.

The ACCA seems more widely used by industry and smaller accountancy practices as the main qualification. This may be in part due to the flexibility of the programme, which offers ten years in which to complete the training and practical experience required. Unlike the straightforward chartered route, ACCA gives students freedom to complete the work experience at any time during the ten years. Other institutes ask for job-based training to be concurrent with the institute training and exams.

SPECIALISED PROFESSIONAL QUALIFICATIONS

In addition to the four main accountancy bodies, two others offer quality, well-used and well-respected qualifications in more specialised areas than general accountancy. These reflect the type of work environments accountants may enter or already be working in, and are broader in scope than the others.

The first is CMA (Certificate in Management Accountancy) from CIMA (Chartered Institute of Management Accountants). As the name suggests, the qualification and course are geared towards those in industry and commerce with a management and business slant. However, CMA students can be found in commerce, financial services, consultancy, government, the public sector and manufacturing. In addition to technical accountancy topics, subjects studied include economics, business law, UK and international standards and organisational management, providing skills in decision-making, management and business strategy and analysis. CIMA does not provide training in audit.

DID YOU KNOW?
The CIMA has a close relationship with the AAT (Association of Accounting Technicians). One in twelve UK students come to CIMA via AAT. (See Chapter 8 for more on AAT.)

The second of the specialised institutes, CIPFA (Chartered Institute of Public Finance and Accountancy) concentrates on providing a postgraduate qualification in financial management for the public sector.

Although CIPFA members are represented throughout local and central government, and in government agencies like the Audit Commission and the NHS, it also has members in the voluntary and private sectors. Skills learnt for the CIPFA qualification, CPFA (Chartered Public Finance Accountant), combined with public sector knowledge, can provide a strong background for any environment with a public sector association.

CIPFA differs slightly from the others as it works closely with the public sector, advising local and central government and researching public sector finance issues.

In fact there is much cross-over between the two specialised qualifications and CIMA and CIPFA training do not limit students to financial management roles in industry or the public sector. Both the CMA and CPFA are respected and widely used.

DID YOU KNOW?
In 2002 CIPFA gave evidence to: the Transport, Local
Government and the Regions Select Committee hearing on
the Draft Local Government Bill; the Committee of the Office
of the Deputy Prime Minister's hearing on the Formula Grant
Distribution for Local Government Finance; and the Scottish
Parliament Inquiry into Prison Estates Review. (CIPFA)

These two qualifications are gaining ground on the ACCA
qualification for providing flexible learning, entrance and business
training. ACCA is the most used qualification internationally. The
real advantage of ACCA is that it has Registered Qualifying Body
status; a big marketing bonus as well as a practical plus. However,
CIPFA is lobbying to achieve the same status so that accountants
with the CPFA qualification can also sign off external audits.

All of the institutes have experienced increases in student
applications in the last few years, with accountancy as a
qualification and as a career growing in popularity. The main
institutes have increased flexibility in learning, enabling many
more women and mature career changers to become interested in
training.

It is obvious in a world of global economics that finance is
becoming an increasingly interesting career subject. The
advantage of professional accountancy qualifications is that due to
the strictly regulated standards of training and practise the UK
institutes and their sponsored qualifications are held in high
esteem around the world. Those with the right letters after their
name are internationally employable.

There are other factors. On the one hand, accountancy has always
had the image of being a steady and stable profession: in an
uncertain job market, young and mature students alike look for job
security. On the other hand, the audit furore surrounding Enron
and Worldcom in the States has given accountancy a more exciting
and influential profile. This has made accountancy seem more
sexy, and young people in particular have looked to the institutes
to find out more.

In an economic world of financial deflation and inflation, the accountant will always have his or her work cut out. Whether the economy is going up and there are mergers and acquisitions to deal with, or whether the economy is on the down-turn and corporate recovery is the main focus, there is always a need for a professional to make sense of the figures, plan financial strategy and ensure that accounts are 'true and fair'.

CHAPTER 7

Choosing postgraduate-level training and work experience

The postgraduate-level courses provided by the institutes are outlined in Chapter 8 but choosing between them is a hard task when there is so much good quality learning and experience on offer.

Often personal circumstances lead to a particular employer or institute. Some institutes provide a list of accredited colleges and employers as a guide for students, but usually the job-based training is sorted out first. Some employers (including the NHS) give students a choice of institute qualification, but most have their own preferences.

Training opportunities are advertised in the local press, on institute websites, on specialist accountancy websites (**see Chapter 11** for details) and through graduate recruitment rounds, which either target universities or promote their schemes through regional graduate fairs. Most employer/institute places for professional qualifications are taken by graduates with good degrees, but there are opportunities for entry at other levels (see below).

More diverse opportunities can be spotted by keeping an eye on the jobs pages in newspapers in your chosen area. Job adverts for trainee positions, as well as those for part-qualified roles (**see Chapter 9** for details) often occur after professional exams have been taken; so key times are January/February and the summer months, following the December and June study periods. Some institutes (like the ICAI – the Institute of Chartered Accountants in Ireland) post vacancies from spring onwards.

THE INSTITUTES

Graduate training courses in larger practices start in September, but the learning on other schemes is flexible and can be picked up at any time of the year, leading to twice-yearly exam opportunities.

Larger public practice firms may not give permission to sit exams in December, when there are pressures in the office due to the Inland Revenue self-assessment deadline.
Amanda Knight, Audit Senior,
Richard Mainwaring, Hereford

Many employers will have preferences for certain qualifications – the Big Four in Britain use ACA (Associate Chartered Accountant) and CA (Chartered Accountant) while smaller practices and public sector organisations prefer ACCA (Associate Certified Chartered Accountant).

For those going into corporate or public finance, the more specific ACMA (Associate Certified Management Accountant) or CPFA (Certified Public Finance Accountant) may open up direct routes into your preferred work environment. Which suits you best is down to what sort of an accountant you'd like to be, or what kind of accountancy job you'd like to have.

Traditional accountants specialising in audit and tax are still required, but this is a shrinking market and is being overtaken by more general accountancy professionals; specialists in specific business areas. If you want audit training (which forms a large part of most of the courses) avoid the CIMA qualification. It omits audit training in favour of specific business skills (see below).

Obviously the broader the course, the wider the choice of career you will have on qualification – those taking the CPFA qualification, for example, usually stay in the public sector.

DID YOU KNOW?
CIPFA (34% of students above 35 years old) and CIMA (25%) have more mature students than the other accountancy institutes.

THE EMPLOYERS

The other, all-important part of the accountancy equation is the sponsoring employer. It is usual – whether in industry, commerce, banking or practice – for the employer to fund the institute training and exams, and provide study leave. Part of the employer's commitment is to provide the appropriate work experience (in standard and content) to support the qualification. This will be monitored by the institute.

Employers work closely with the institutes to provide the right kind of work experience, on-the-job tuition and guidance needed by the student. Institutes approve the employers they work with and give students access to approved employers via job vacancies on websites. Look at the institute websites under careers or employers when starting out.

I liked the idea of a large firm with the option of working in different departments. I was given the opportunity to work in the New York office in my first year of training, helping on the completion of an acquisition for a client in Edinburgh.

Forbes Johnston, PricewaterhouseCoopers, Edinburgh*

*Courtesy of ICAS

Where you work and train can be decided by a number of factors.

1. What type of work environment do you want to work in?
   Choose from:
   - Public practice (accountancy firms)
   - Industry (manufacturing, engineering, service)
   - Public sector (local government, central government)
   - Financial institutions (banks, insurance companies)
   - Charities and NGOs (non-government organisations).

The majority of training places in the UK are offered in the first three categories.

2. What size organisation do you want to work in?
   - Large – international corporations, organisations, government agencies or practices (like the Big Four), where there is strong competition for training graduate places, but where a variety of opportunities may be on offer
   - Medium-sized – companies, organisations and practices that may not expect the sparkling academic record demanded by larger employers and where you will work alongside a smaller group of trainees. The work may be more specific and you may gain knowledge in a specialist area
   - Small – companies, organisations and practices where you will be among only a handful of trainees, or maybe the only one at a particular office or branch. Trainees are chosen on a broader basis and previous work experience is sometimes given more consideration than an impressive degree. You may be able to make your mark more easily in a small office.

3. Geography – your priority may be to work and train in a particular area

4. Contacts – sometimes it's who you know, not what you know!

In order to be accepted for a training position with an employer and to qualify for entry to the institute courses, students will have to meet certain criteria. The institutes' entry criteria are listed below, but what an employer wants is more specific.

Some employers stipulate a degree in accountancy, economics or business, while others ask for honours degree holders only. Competition may be so fierce for prestigious places that only those with a First will win an interview.

When recruiting graduates we invest a lot of time finding out about individuals. This is based on academic record, a thorough testing process, behavioural interviews and a detailed look at any work experience.
Stevan Rolls, Director, Resourcing and Employee Integration, Ernst & Young

There's no getting around the fact that academic achievement is the primary factor considered by recruiting employers in this country. This may be proven by degree status or by professional qualification. Those who enter at a vocational level **(see Chapter 8)** will have to prove academic ability and work-based knowledge by passing professional exams at a pre-grauate or graduate level before moving on to the chartered qualification.

Each employer has pros and cons and it ultimately comes down to whether you like them and they like you. The three to ten years you may spend as a trainee accountant (whatever qualification) will be hard work, so you must enjoy where you work and the work you do, and have the determination to do your best at work and at study. The pressure of combining work and exam study at this level – regardless of home life or a social life – requires determination and commitment.

You've got to be completely dedicated to making a career out of accountancy. There's no way around studying hard and sitting exams.
Tim Brown, Trainee Chartered Accountant, Burton Sweet, Bristol

TRAINING OPTIONS

ACA QUALIFICATION

The ICAEW (Institute of Certified Accountants in England and Wales) is the largest body offering a Certified Accountancy qualification. The ACA is one of the longest established and most revered qualifications; it's at the top of the tree.

Although in the past the ACA has been accused of being rigid, over-formal and old-fashioned, in recent years the ICAEW has taken a fresh view. The institute and the qualification have become brighter, less fuddy-duddy and more tuned in to future accountancy needs, rather than expectations of the past.

The ACA has been reviewed and developed in recent years to offer a more realistic way of learning based on everyday business needs, and underpinning technical skills. An improvement in student access to learning, with a new work-based learning process and more online support, has contributed to beefing up the ACA in competition with its excellent rivals.

The appeal of the ACA is that it has a long-established kudos and is regarded as producing the crème de la crème of chartered accountants in Britain.

DID YOU KNOW?
One in eight ACAs lives and works overseas. (ICAEW)

Entry requirements and exemptions for the ACA:

- **18 year olds** with A or B grades in GCSE Maths and English, plus a UCAS score of 220 or equivalent. (The ICAEW is more interested in high grades at A-level than any particular subject)

- **Degree holders** must have at least a 2:2, but 76% of ICAEW graduate trainees have a first or a 2:1. Only 4% of ACA graduates studied Accountancy at degree level, but those who have taken relevant courses may be exempt from some exams in the first stage of the qualification

- **Qualified AATs (Associate Accounting Technicians)** are exempt from the Accounting and Law parts of the Professional Level of the course. There is a Fast Track scheme for those in their second year of AAT. Students in the AAT Technician stage can take the ACA Top Up paper and go on to start the ICAEW Professional Stage. Once successfully completed, the student is awarded the PAQ (Professional Accountancy Certificate) before entering the final Advanced stage of the ACA. **See Chapter 8** for more information on Accounting Technician qualifications.

The ACA course runs concurrently with a three-year training contract and is broken down into two main parts: the Professional Stage (which provides a grounding in the concepts and principles of accounting); and the Advanced Stage, which deals with, the practical application of technical knowledge.

ACA syllabus:

Professional	Advanced
Exams:	*Exams:*
Accounting	Test of Advanced Technical
Audit and Assurance	Competence
Business Finance	*Assessments:*
Business Management	Advanced Case Study
Financial Reporting	
Taxation	
Assessments in:	
Commercial and Company Law	

CA QUALIFICATION

The ICAS (Institute of Chartered Accountants of Scotland) provides a similar course to the ACA. The institute now has a London office and you don't have to be resident in Scotland to apply. Many English practices and companies support the CA qualification.

DID YOU KNOW?
Fifty-nine per cent of CAs work in industry and commerce. Of those in public practice, nearly half work at Partnership level. (ICAS)

The ICAS has many attractions, including exclusive use of the Chartered Accountant (CA) status, a proven track record (over 130 years), a standard training contract of three years (the shortest time it takes to complete the CA) and the opportunity to develop specialisms during the second and third year of training.

Entry requirements and exemptions for the CA:

- **18 year olds** with A-levels or Highers in Maths and English or with any equivalent qualification from Northern Ireland or the Republic of Ireland can apply. However, at least 22 UCAS points in total are required

- **Graduates** with a good degree in any subject can apply. Degree holders will be assessed individually, and if they have undertaken appropriate past study (which may include accounting or business elements) they may be exempt from some or all of the five exams at Test of Competence

- **AAT qualifications** will go towards entry requirements for the CA. Those who want to study for the AAT from scratch can expect to qualify at CA level within a minimum of five years. **See Chapter 8** for more information on Accounting Technician qualifications

- Those holding other **institute qualifications** will be individually assessed for exemption.

The CA has high pass rates, which may be due to the fact that ICAS is the only institute that trains as well as sets the exams – a way in which ICAS can stay in tune with student learning.

The CA qualification requires passes at all levels in the exams and the work-based competencies. The study is classroom-based and takes place in 15 centres in Britain. These are: Aberdeen, Birmingham, Bristol, Cambridge, Dundee, Edinburgh, Glasgow, Leeds, London, Luton, Manchester, Newcastle, Nottingham, Reading and Southampton.

The syllabus contains ten subjects leading to three stages of examination: The Test of Competence (TC) – acquisition of knowledge base; the Test of Professional Skills (TPS) – development of practical skills; and the Test of Professional Expertise (TPE) – judgement.

CA Syllabus

Test of Competence	Financial Accounting	Business Law	Business Management	Principles of Auditing and Reporting	Finance
Test of Professional Skills	Financial Reporting	Assurance and Business Systems	Taxation	Advanced Finance	
Test of Professional Expertise	Multi-discipline case study				

The syllabus below is correct as at August 2003.

Test of Competence					
Financial Accounting	Conceptual basis of accounting	Introduction to financial statements	Recording transactions	Business Structures	Preparation of accounts
Business Law	Introduction to law	Formation of companies and record	Share and loan capital	Administration of the company	Contract and commercial law
Business Law	Negligence	Insolvency	Trusts	Intellectual property	
Business Management	Organisation structures	Businesses processes	Business information	Cost accounting	Pricing strategies
Business Management	Budgetary planning and control	Quantitative techniques	Contribution analysis	Performance Measurements	Working capital management
Principles of auditing and reporting	Principles of third party assurance	Objectives and evidence	Approaches to audit assignments	Responsibilities of the auditor	Audit Regulation in the UK
Principles of auditing and reporting	Introduction to the corporate reporting framework				
Finance	Finance function and environment	Securities and markets	Capital market models	Financial analysis	Financial forecasting and planning
Finance	Capital investment appraisal	Personal finance			

The syllabus below is correct as at December 2003

Test of professional skills					
Financial Reporting	Generally accepted accounting principles	Accounting for business transactions	Single company financial statements	Group financial statements	Corporate reporting
Assurance and Business Systems	The audit and assurance process	Business risk	Control environment	regulation	Systems management
Assurance and Business Systems	Electronic markets				
Taxation	Introduction to taxation	Principles of computing trading	Income tax	Corporation tax	VAT
Taxation	National Insurance	Inheritance Tax	Capital Gains Tax	Professional conduct	
Advanced Finance	Short term financial management	Long term financial policy	Advanced capital investment	Company valuations, mergers and acquisitions	Financial distress
Advanced Finance	Equity markets	Banks	Corporate debt securities	Loan documentation	Derivatives – swaps, forward, futures and options
Advanced Finance	Regulatory environment and professional conduct	Impact of national economic policy			

The syllabus below is correct as at November 2004.

Test of Professional Expertise					
Multi-discipline Case Study	Corporate plan	Corporate strategies and management	Business improvement	Management of financial structures	Ethics

The CA qualification extends far beyond accountancy. It has enabled me to tackle everything from headline-grabbing corporate finance transactions in public practice to strategic decision-making in one of the world's largest entertainment companies.

Alison Cornwell, Walt Disney TV International*
*Courtesy of ICAS

Work experience for the CA is carried out with an ICAS-approved employer. ICAS says that every year there are over 800 vacancies in over 200 training offices in the UK.

The work-based learning is assessed on a range of competencies. Progess on these is recorded in an Achievement Log that's kept over the three-year placement. Experience gained at work will depend on the type of employer, but there are fundamental competencies that have to be achieved.

The prescribed competencies are: Accountancy (financial and management); Information Technology; Communication Skills; and Personal Skills. Optional competencies could include: Management Consultancy; Corporate Finance; Corporate Recovery; Treasury Management; Corporate Taxation; Information Systems; Auditing; Financial Reporting; and Business Finance. At the end of the first year of training the student and employer agree a minimum of a further five competencies to be achieved in the second and third years.

The aim of this combination of competencies is to ensure the student covers the essential work experience expected by ICAS, and gains specialist knowledge in the areas particular to the employer. This gives the student practical and usable skills and satisfies the employer's need for an active and involved employee – after all, it is the employer who pays for the training!

ACA QUALIFICATION FROM ICAI

The ICAI (Institute of Chartered Accountants in Ireland) also has an ACA qualification. Like its British cousin, the Irish ACA requires a minimum of three years' supervised work experience, passes in professional exams set by the institute, and, in addition, competence in information technology. This is achieved through the Personal Computing for Accountants assessment.

In Ireland, training in practice remains the more popular path – training in business has only been on offer since 1983 – and there are many more vacancies in firms than in industry. However, the financial services sector and banking welcome a proportion of students and qualifieds.

DID YOU KNOW?
The ICAI is the biggest employer of graduates in Ireland – 95% of the entrants into training (for the Irish ACA) enter as graduates. (ICAI)

Entry requirements and exemptions for the Irish ACA:

- **Graduates with a good degree** in any subject can apply, although more accountancy and business graduates apply than graduates in general subjects. Degree holders will be assessed individually, and if they have undertaken appropriate past study (which may include accounting or business elements), they may be exempt from some of the Professional (Two and Three) exams. Those without any prior learning will have to attend an introductory programme in Basic Accounting

- **Postgraduates** with recognised one-year Master's or Diplomas in Accounting are exempt from Professional Two and Three exams but have to complete the three years work experience

- **Students with the IATI (institute of Accounting Technicans in Ireland) Foundation exam (with Distinction)** can start with the ICAI Professional Two exam. Students enter a five-and-a-half-year training programme in order to achieve the ACA

- Those holding other **accounting institute qualifications** will be individually assessed for exemptions.

The three exams for the ACA are: Professional Two; Professional Three; and the Final Admitting Examination. Some students will have to begin by studying a foundation-level programme in Basic Accounting.

ICAI ACA

Foundation	Professional Two	Professional Three	Final Admitting Examination
Basic Accounting	Financial Accounting	Advanced Financial Accounting	Test of competence in:
	Business Information Systems	Auditing	Auditing and the Reporting Accountant
	Management Accounting and Business Finance1	Management Accounting and Business Finance2	Financial Accounting and Reporting
	Taxation1	Taxation2	Tax Planning
	Stand Alone Company Law module		Management Accounting
			Business Finance
			Business Strategy
			Business Strategy
			Business Ethics
			Information Management

In addition, students have to complete Personal Computing for Accountants, which is a study-based IT programme. The remainder of the training is provided in the workplace and by CAS (the Centre of Accounting Studies), which provides lectures, assignments, mock examinations, classes and workshops across the island.

The combination of C & C's management programmes and the Chartered Accountant exams has given me an excellent grounding in commercial management.
Trevor Lydon, Group Finance Analyst, Cantrell and Cochrane Group Ltd

ACCA QUALIFICATION

Slightly different to the above three is the ACCA (Association of Chartered Certified Accountants) qualification, also called ACCA (Associate Chartered Certified Accountant).

This qualification is newer than the others: until 1974 (when chartered status was bestowed on ACCA) it was the only available certified qualification. Since then ACCA has become the fastest growing accountancy institute in the world.

The advantage of the ACCA qualification is that you have ten years to complete the training and exams. It may seem like a long time but with changes in circumstances – like work developments, travel abroad, maternity leave, or even just having to re-take exams – it is useful to be able to take your time. I know some people who have gone down the chartered route and have run out of time.
Amanda Knight, Audit Senior, Richard Mainwaring, Hereford

Many companies choose the ACCA as it offers students more flexibility at entry level and various choices for learning. Extensive online tuition is available as well as a network of colleges around the world. ACCA also provides the opportunity for students to complete the three-year job experience at a different time to the exams – either before or after, as long as it is within a ten year period.

DID YOU KNOW?
There are over 200 ACCA examination centres in more than 140 countries around the world. (ACCA)

Entry requirements and exemptions for ACCA:

- **18 year olds** with two A-levels and three GCSEs in a total of five separate subjects including Maths and English Language, or any equivalent qualification from Scotland, Northern Ireland or the Republic of Ireland can apply

- **Mature students over 21** need no prior experience or qualifications and applicants are assessed individually. However, mature students have just two years (four consecutive exam sessions) to pass Part 1 papers 1.1 and 1.2

- **Degree holders** will be assessed individually and if they have undertaken appropriate past study (which may include accounting or business elements) they may be exempt from some or all of Part 1 and 2 exams

- Those holding other **institute qualifications** will be individually assessed for exemptions

- **Certified Accounting Technicians** (minimum age 16) who have completed Level C of the ACCA's Certified Accounting Technician qualification are exempt from Part 1. **See Chapter 8** for more information on Accounting Technician qualifications

- **Association of Accounting Technicians** (AAT) members who have completed Intermediate and Technician levels are exempt from papers 1.1 and 1.2.

The ACCA course is divided into three parts

Part 1	Part 2	Part 3
Basic accounting principles Financial information Key managerial issues	Core technical skills Business legislation Key accounting skills	Strategic management Information evaluation and consultancy Key employment technical skills

Overview of ACCA syllabus:

Part 1	Part 2	Part 3 Any two from:	Part 3 All core papers:
1.1 Preparing financial statements	2.1 Information systems	3.1 Auditing and assurance services	3.5 Strategic business planning and development
1.2 Financial information for management	2.2 Corporate and business law	3.2 Advanced taxation	3.6 Advanced corporate reporting
1.3 Managing people	2.3 Business taxation	3.3 Performance management	3.7 Strategic financial management
	2.4 Financial management and control	3.4 Business information management	
	2.5 Financial reporting		
	2.6 Audit and internal review		

The practical experience part of the qualification is organised with an employment supervisor. Students have to keep a Student Training Record to log their achievements. This can form the beginning of an ongoing Personal Development Plan (PDP).

Core subjects in Part 3 are mandatory, but other choices of study give students a chance to gear the course towards an individual's work environment.

Those who think that ACCA is a softer option than the other institutes' qualifications need to think again. During the course

ACCA students sit 14 three-hour exams twice a year in June and December. A maximum of four papers can be taken at each sitting. Part 3 core papers have to be taken and passed in the same session, but ACCA counts credits successfully gained for Parts 1 and 2, which prevents unnecessary re-taking of exams.

ACMA QUALIFICATION

ACMA (Associate Member of the Chartered Institute of Management Accountants) is the first of the Specialised Accountancy postgraduate-level professional qualifications. It is distinct from all other chartered accountancy qualifications in that it does not include training in external audit but offers a broader-based business and finance syllabus.

DID YOU KNOW?
There are more than 20,000 companies worldwide employing CIMA students. In Britain the biggest employer of CIMA trainees is the NHS, with 900 students, followed by PricewaterhouseCoopers Consulting. (CIMA)

The ACMA is delivered by the CIMA (Chartered Institute of Management Accountants) and is taken in three parts: Foundation, Intermediate and Final. The qualification is well established and widely used in industry, commerce and practice where there is no emphasis on audit. The course encompasses key decision-making, management, strategy, and analysis, as well as finance skills. Key activities are related to Business Strategy, Information Strategy and Finance Strategy.

The Certificate was a slog to achieve, but home study suited me. It took nearly four years to complete the training and take the exams, but it was worth it. The training gave me a good starting point. I still use the knowledge and expertise today.
Susannah Hamilton, Finance Manager, European Engineering Company, England

CIMA members are not trained in audit, which leaves room for allied business subjects such as human resources, knowledge management and marketing. Consequently, CIMA members don't always work in finance departments. Many can be found in management consulting, business analysis, or project management within an organisation.

Entry requirements and exemptions for CIMA:

- **18 year olds** with two A-levels (grades A–E) and three GCSEs (grades A–C), including Maths and English Language, or any equivalent qualification from Scotland, Northern Ireland or the Republic of Ireland can apply

- **Mature students aged 25 or over** need no academic qualifications but must be working in an accounting environment. Proof of English Language and Maths skills, along with a description of general job duties, are required from an employer in order to qualify

- **Degree holders** will be assessed individually, and if they have undertaken appropriate past study they may be exempt from some exams. There are three new Graduate Fast Track schemes and entry requirements for these can be accessed on the CIMA website **(see Chapter 11)**

- Those holding other **institute qualifications** will be individually assessed for exemptions

- Those who have successfully completed the **AAT Technician Stage** (including the Central Assessment or Final Level exams) are granted exemptions from all five of CIMA's Foundation Level subjects. **See Chapter 8** for more information on Accounting Technician qualifications

- Those with the **Open University Certificate in Accounting (see Chapter 8)** are granted exemptions from all five of CIMA's Foundation Level subjects.

Overview of CIMA syllabus

Foundation	Intermediate	Final
1. Financial Accounting Fundamentals	4. Finance	12. Management accounting – business strategy
2. Management accounting fundamentals	5. Business Taxation	13. Management accounting – financial strategy
3a Economics for Business	6a Financial Accounting – UK standards OR 6b Financial accounting – International standards	14. Management accounting – information strategy
3b Business law	7a Financial reporting – UK standards (IFRP) OR 7b Financial reporting – International standards	15. Management accounting – case study
3c Business mathematics	8. Management Accounting – performance management	
	9. Management accounting – decision-making	
	10. Systems and project management	
	11. Organisational management	

The CIMA Foundation, Intermediate and Final exams take place in May and November each year. The CIMA is not a tuition provider and there is no requirement to participate in formal learning to enter the exams; however, the CIMA website lists suitable courses to help with study. (**See Chapter 11** for contact details of all the institutes.) These vary from part-time to weekend and revision courses. Learning is easier if you can take part in a study programme; alternatively, there is the option of distance learning with a tutorial link. For those who want to go it alone there is a home study manual that students work through in the lead up to exams.

DID YOU KNOW?
At any one time there are 73,000 people studying for CIMA qualifications around the world. (CIMA)

CPFA QUALIFICATION

The second of the Specialised Accountancy qualifications is the CPFA (Chartered Public Finance Accountant) provided by CIPFA (Chartered Institute of Public Finance and Accountancy).

The CPFA provides coverage of accountancy topics similar to the other chartered courses – including audit – but adds public sector subjects. The main difference between this qualification and the others is the specialist element of Public Policy. This provides specific knowledge for those working in any public sector environment, from local government to housing associations and higher education.

CIPFA is applying for Registered Qualifying Body status, which would enable accountants with CPFA to sign off external audits.

An open learning system forms the basis for the course. This is given online and via home study packages, with telephone helpline support. It is not necessary for a student to spend time at a study centre, but there is the option of 30 days' attendance for each professional stage, taken as day release or week release, plus a short revision course.

Course centres are at: Birmingham, Bristol, Dublin, Durham, Chelmsford, Edinburgh, Glasgow, Lisburn, Liverpool, London, Nottingham and Pontypridd.

CIPFA's high quality open learning system is easy to follow and makes studying enjoyable. It helped me to pass all my exams first time – and I'm no Einstein!

Jim Rooney, Head of Finance and Administration, Berwickshire Housing Association

Entry requirements and exemptions for CPFA:

- **18 year olds** with two A-levels and three GCSEs (grades A–C), including Maths and English Language, or BTEC and SCOTVEC National Certificates and NVQs and SVQs at Level Three, or any equivalent qualification from Scotland, Northern Ireland or the Republic of Ireland can apply

- **Mature entrants over 21** with three years' relevant work experience can start at Foundation Level

- **Senior entrants aged 25 and over** with five years' relevant work experience are exempt from Foundation Level exams

- **Degree holders** will be assessed individually, according to appropriate past study. Those with an Accounting degree may be exempt from all or part of the Foundation and Part 1 exams. Those with HNC or HND Business and Finance or HNC or HND Accounting are exempt from the Foundation level

- Those holding other **institute qualifications** will be individually assessed for exemptions. Professional Accountants with chartered status can gain the CPFA qualification in a minimum of nine months

- **Associate Accounting Technicians** are exempt from the Foundation Level and part of Part 1. **See Chapter 8** for more information on Accounting Technician qualifications.

Any passes are held for two years, but retakes of failed modules must be taken within a two-year period.

The work experience part of the qualification is undertaken with an approved company in the public sector. Professional 3 is where the practical application of the theory learnt in other stages of the CPFA is tested in two ways. The project part takes the form of a thesis directly relating to the employer, while the objective of the Finance and Management Case Study Examination is to: 'test the application of acquired skills . . . to put candidates in, as near as possible, a practical office situation and test reaction under a time constraint'.

Overview of CPFA syllabus

Foundation	Professional 1	Professional 2	Professional 3
Financial Accounting	Accounting Theory and Practice	Financial Reporting and Accountability	Final Test of Professional Competence:
Cost Accounting and Quantitative Analysis	Management Accounting	Accounting for Decision Making	Finance and Management Case Study Examination
Law and Effective Management	Audit	Public Policy and Taxation	Project – a thesis of 5,000-6,000 words on a topic of practical value to the employing organisation
	Information and Financial Management	Business Strategy and Management	

DID YOU KNOW?
CIPFA student registrations have increased for four consecutive years (2003). (CIPFA)

All of the six chartered qualifications outlined in this chapter are well established, high quality and renowned professional qualifications; they are all academic in nature and require work experience in conjunction with course-based study. Which one you choose depends on your career aspirations, personal interests, talents, circumstances and employment opportunities.

NON-PROFESSIONAL POSTGRADUATE TRAINING

There are Accountancy and Business Master's degrees and Diplomas available in the UK for graduates with good degrees who want to pursue the research side of accountancy and finance.

Although a student can steer an academic path towards a doctorate, these postgraduate courses do not confer the title Professional Accountant (with chartered status) unless one of the institute qualifications has already been achieved.

A postgraduate degree, however, will entitle the holder to exemptions on some of the institute exams, depending on coursework covered.

MBAs (Master of Business Administration) for accountants are becoming increasingly popular as finance employees hone their management and business skills in preparation for senior positions.

CHAPTER 8

Graduate and pre-graduate-level qualifications

Every organisation and every kind of organisation has to have someone overseeing the financial implications of the business. For those that are not large enough for their own finance department – sole traders for instance – the accountancy practice provides the service. For the very large organisation, internal finance departments as well as accountancy and consultancy firms provide everything from payroll provision to insolvency advice.

At every step of the way, from collecting accounts information to standardising procurement and working out VAT, there will be employees whose job it is to collate, manage and communicate information. These finance employees may not have an institute qualification, or they may be working towards one over a number of years. Their roles are important and with new corporate legislation, financial safeguards and tax changes, they are much needed.

Although many may aspire to Professional Accountant level – and graduate applications are on the increase – an estimated 800,000 people in the UK are working in accounting and finance without any qualification (AAT survey).

Although many employees have a wealth of job experience and have picked up some training along the way, those who do have some form of recognised training and professional learning find themselves more marketable, especially when starting at the bottom of the career ladder.

Traditionally, it has been the academic high-flyers who have taken 'articles' and have gone into accountancy, but there are many interesting and challenging roles in accounting and finance open to anyone without chartered status.

VOCATIONAL TRAINING

Until the 1980s, when it was recognised that standardised training at different levels was needed, there were only two ways to obtain a recognised qualification – chartered or certified. Even now there are many accounting employees who have not yet found training and learning to suit their career needs.

Although more vocational training is now on offer, most of the institutes have yet to develop a modern apprenticeship – only ACCA and AAT offer training at NVQ Level 2 or 3 – an obvious way to meet both employers' and employees' needs and to fill skills gaps.

The CIMA has recognised that not everyone wants to aim for ACMA status and has re-marketed its qualifications so that passes of the foundation level merit a Certificate in Business Accounting, and those at Intermediate level gain an advanced Diploma in Management Accounting.

DID YOU KNOW?
According to *Skills in England* (a report from the Learning and Skills Council), 23% of all companies suffered skills gaps in 2002 (an increase of 7% from 2001). In particular, there was a 17% skills gap in finance and business services.

The skills that are lacking are often seen as 'hard' – such as computer software or accounting technical knowledge – and employees can be put through training to remedy the gap. But more often it's the 'soft' skills – like communication, negotiation and project management – that are missing, and these come not just from learning, but from confidence and experience too. The right kind of working environment, as well as the right kind of courses, are needed in order for people to get the best out of continued learning.

In many instances the gap appears the biggest at middle management and below. The Skills Council report indicates that half of the 16% of employees in the finance and business sector are in clerical or administrative positions. This workforce would most benefit from 'on-the-job' training.

ACCOUNTING TECHNICIANS

The AAT (Association of Accounting Technicians) is a different institute to the six discussed so far, but it has close links with the other bodies and is sponsored by four of them: ICAEW, ICAS, CIMA and CIPFA. It offers accountancy and bookkeeping qualifications, which provide a second tier of learning – at non-graduate vocational level – to accountancy training.

Established in 1980, the AAT provides a recognised professional qualification for accounting technicians and now has over 100,000 members worldwide. In comparison to the other institutes, the AAT courses are recently developed and popular with employers, students and accountancy bodies.

Accounting technicians work in a variety of jobs in public and private sectors and in accountancy practice. Positions range from Accounts Clerk or Bookkeeper to Financial Controller or Director of Finance.

DID YOU KNOW?
Salary surveys show that AAT qualified accounting technicians can earn up to 24% more than their non-qualified counterparts. (Accountancy Additions 2002)

The AAT offers accounting qualifications at three levels:

1. Foundation (equivalent to NVQ/SVQ Level 2) – six compulsory units

2. Intermediate (equivalent to NVQ/SVQ Level 3) – four compulsory units

3. Technician (equivalent to NVQ/SVQ Level 4) – three compulsory units.

Students also have to choose one of four units on the drafting of financial statements, plus three other optional units. The compulsory units on computing, and health and safety at work, can be taken at any stage.

Each level is an individual qualification, so students do not have to complete the three to receive a certificate and gain a recognised standard.

The AAT has set up courses to make the qualifications open to anyone over school-leaving age, and learning is via a variety of providers. There is no time limit for completion, although the minimum expected completion for the first two stages is a year for each, plus two years for Technician level. Work experience is not part of the qualification, but an employer could provide AAT training in-house.

The Foundation year helped with the business – I learnt about holiday pay for instance. Apart from practical applications, it gives you a good grounding in accounting. I learnt the old system of T Accounts, which is manual bookkeeping. Although I wouldn't use it day-to-day, if the computer goes down I can resort to manual.

Julie Pullen, AAT Intermediate, Gloucestershire

Overview of AAT syllabus:

Foundation NVQ/SVQ Level 2 Accounting	Intermediate NVQ/SVQ Level 3 Accounting
Recording income and receipts	Maintaining financial records and preparing accounts
Making and recording payments	Recording and evaluating costs and revenues
Preparing ledger balances and initial trial balance	Preparing reports and returns
Supplying information for management control	Working with computers (if not completed at Level 2)
Working with computers	Contributing to the maintenance of a healthy, safe and productive working environment (if not completed at Level 2)
Achieving personal affectiveness	
Contributing to the maintenance of a healthy, safe and productive working environment	

Technician NVQ/SVQ Level 4 Accounting		
Compulsory units	Plus any two of these four:	Plus any one of these four:
Contributing to the management of performance and the enhancement of value	Operating a cash and credit control system	Drafting financial statements (accounting practice, industry and commerce)
Contributing to the planning and control of resources	Implementing auditing procedures	Drafting financial statements (Central Government)
Managing systems and people in the accounting environment	Preparing business taxation computations	Drafting financial statements (Local Government)
Contributing to the maintenance of a healthy, safe and productive working environment (if not completed at another Level)	Preparing personal taxation computations	Drafting financial statements (National Health Service)

The Foundation course provides core bookkeeping skills, the Intermediate course provides an introduction to accounting and the Technician course, in addition to accounting and finance systems, gives the student the choice of specialist knowledge aimed at different job markets – industry and commerce, central government, local government and the NHS.

DID YOU KNOW?
One in ten students applying for the CIMA qualification comes via the AAT route. (CIMA)

In addition to the AAT Accounting Technician courses, the institute also provides: AAT Bookkeeping Certificate (ABC); NVQ/SVQ in Payroll Administration at levels 2 and 3; and an AAT Diploma in Government Finance, specifically for central government employees.

ACCA ACCOUNTING TECHNICIAN QUALIFICATION (CAT)

ACCA has launched its own new accounting technician qualification similar to the AAT's but with the additional element of on-the-job training. The CAT (Certified Accounting Technician) is based on the institute's usual mix of study and practical experience and builds knowledge in accountancy, IT and management.

Although the new qualification is yet unproven – the first exams will take place in 2004 – it looks to have immense appeal, with flexibility and accessibility its strong selling points.

Qualification is not restricted by any time limit, although minimum completion time is one year. Unusually, exams can be taken in a subject order that fits in with an individual student's work experience, subject to ACCA's timetable. Some exams are computer-based, so students don't have to attend college for every examination.

Importantly, with new international standards in accounting looming, CAT offers the option of studying for either international or UK accounting and auditing standards.

Entry is open to anyone of school-leaving age and over – regardless of exam passes – while for mature entrants, relevant qualifications are taken into account for exam and study exemptions.

Entry requirements and exemptions for CAT:

- CAT qualification gives eligibility to transfer to the ACCA professional scheme and exempts the holder from Part 1 exams

- The qualification is open to anyone over the age of 16

- Older students with work experience or relevant qualifications qualify for exemptions to exams.

Overview of CAT syllabus:

Paper 1 Recording Financial Transactions (International or British standards)	Paper 6 Drafting Financial Statements International or British Standards)
Paper 2 Information for Management Control	Part 7 Planning, Control and Performance Management
Paper 3 Maintaining Financial Records (International or British Standards)	Part 8 Implementing Audit Procedures (International or British Standards)
Paper 4 Accounting Costs	Part 9 Preparing Taxation Computations
Paper 5 Managing People and Systems	Part 10 Managing Finances

OPEN UNIVERSITY CERTIFICATE IN ACCOUNTING

The OU Certificate in Accounting is a one-year course leading to the Cert.Acc. (Open). For students interested in further management qualifications, it also grants access to the Professional Diploma in Management and then to Stage Two of the MBA.

As with all OU courses, it is taken by distance learning and there are no prerequisite entry requirements. For anyone interested in gaining more accounting knowledge, but who doesn't want to commit to an institute qualification, this is a good taster or stepping-stone. Once completed, it provides some exemptions to institute exams if students want to take accountancy further.

ACCOUNTANCY AND ACCOUNTING DEGREES

In the past decade, there has been an increase in vocational degrees with a variety of specialist modules on offer in addition to general subjects. For those who at 18 know they want to go into business, and who also want to go to university, business-tailored courses provide a glimpse of different areas of life in industry and commerce. The advantage of business-related courses is that students can make an educated choice about employment when they graduate.

A number of degrees in business or management and accounting are available in the UK.

Accounting and business graduates will be exempt from some accountancy institute exams if they have studied certain subjects (e.g. corporate law), but these exemptions only occur in the first or second stage of the institutes' qualifications.

The main benefit of a specialist degree is the background knowledge and insight gained from studying related subjects at university when approaching the professional qualification.

For those budding accountants who also want degrees, however, it is of no great advantage to study accounting at university. This may seem an odd comment to make, but because accountancy is such an old profession with well-established training routes, in order to become a Professional Accountant, a relevant qualification from an institute has to be obtained in addition to any accountancy-related degree. An accountancy degree – unlike a law degree – does not start you off on a recognised professional path.

Accountancy	Accounting	Accounting & Finance	Accounting & Financial Management	Accounting & Management
Dundee	Bournemouth	Aberystwyth Birmingham Brighton De Montfort (Leicester) East Anglia	Loughbor- ough	Aston (Birmingham)
Northumbria	Cardiff Essex	Essex Glamorgan Kent Kingston	Sheffield	Cardiff
	Hertfordshire	Lancaster Leeds Leeds Metropolitan Liverpool John Moores		
	Hull	London Guildhall London School of Economics Manchester		
	Liverpool	Manchester Metro Northumbria Nottingham Nottingham Trent Oxford Brookes Plymouth		
	Portsmouth Sheffield Hallam	Salford Southampton South Bank (London) West of England		

Accounting & Business	Business & Accounting	Economics & Accounting	Economics & Accountancy	Management Sciences and Accounting
De Montfort (Leicester)	Exeter	Bristol	City (London)	Southampton
Sunderland			Reading	

Institute-recommended degree subjects range from History and Archaeology to Biology and Economics. These teach the student to think analytically, which is a key accountancy skill.

It's worth remembering that employers and institutes put an emphasis on the quality of degree rather than subject matter in the entry requirements for Professional Accountancy training.

Because top training places are so competitive and institute standards are so high, only those with a first or 2:1 stand a chance of a graduate place with the Big Four. Even those looking for placements with smaller practices or in industry will have to achieve good degrees: the ICAEW, ICAS and ICAI all demand proof of academic prowess when recruiting.

BUSINESS ACCOUNTING AND FINANCE BA (HONS), NEWCASTLE

There are usually exceptions to general rules and there is one university degree course that is not only approved by the ICAEW (Institute of Chartered Accountants in England and Wales), but also sponsored by it. It's new and it's a degree with a difference. The Business Accounting and Finance BA (Hons) is a vocational programme, which includes work placement throughout the course.

The ICAEW partnered with PricewaterhouseCoopers and the University of Newcastle upon Tyne support the degree programme, which was launched in September 2002.

As with most 'sandwich' courses, the degree is a four-year programme but it includes paid work placements in years two, three and four. The course has been designed to cover subjects in the ICAEW ACA (Associate Chartered Accountant) Professional Stage Syllabus and the devolved assessments in Law.

So far the course has been over-subscribed and places are well contested. Entry requires a high standard of academic achievement at the age of 18. Typical offers are based on three A-level grades of A, A and B (320 UCAS tariff points).

This special sandwich has the advantage of providing an honours degree qualification, combined with relevant work experience, and professional accountancy qualification coursework and standards.

The first students have not yet completed the degree so there are no assessments of the course's success yet, but it looks like being an undergraduate training template for the future.

CHAPTER 9

Starting out

Accountancy opportunities in the UK peaked in 2000 and 2001. Since then companies have reduced trainee places to fit the downward economic market and to cut company costs. With more young people waking up to the possibilities of accountancy, those starting at the very beginning may have a competitive time ahead. Whether you're 16, 18 or 21, you need to think about how you are going to become the best possible candidate.

If you are looking ahead to a future in accountancy and have not yet left school or obtained the qualifications you need to train, now is the time to consider what you need to develop and learn in the intervening period.

Competition for places at top accountancy firms providing professional training is high, and although you may not want to work for the Big Four practices in the country – or even the slightly smaller 20 – it's worth considering their requirements for recruits. Alongside a proven academic record and good interpersonal and communication skills, training and development departments require:

● Relevant work experience in an accountancy/finance environment – this can be brief, like a summer internship for instance.

- Any work experience that demonstrates good communication skills and team work. If you are interested in specialising in one sector (public, industry or charity for example) relevant work experience in that area is helpful

- The constructive use of holiday time and a gap year – back-packing around Thailand may give you some Brownie points but needs to be balanced with other productive activities

- Travelling that shows independence, maturity and resourcefulness – a week in Ibiza doesn't count!

- Club or charity involvement – from sport and music to looking after kids – to show you have balanced a useful social life with work and study. Active involvement in an organisation on a voluntary or social basis (e.g. the Student Union) will score you extra points

- An interest in the business world. Prove you are up to date with key international business and economic issues and you're on to a winner

- Enthusiasm. This is last, but definitely not least. You have to be 100% convinced of what you want to do and be able to explain why.

Of course, not everyone wants to enter accountancy at the same level, in the same way and via the same firms. Only a small percentage of accountancy applicants get into the Big Four training schemes, but the above expectations are ones that many other employers may consider in addition to exam passes.

Whether it's an AAT course you're applying for or postgraduate training, when an employer invests a maximum of five years' training plus study leave and tuition fees, it wants to make sure it's getting the right person for the job.

CHOOSING TRAINING

Choosing training is not just down to finding the course that will get you where you want to go, or the employer that will have you!

Training at any level for any qualification is a huge commitment and you need to make sure it's the right course of action for you as well as the right course.

So how do you match a training scheme with:

1. Your present qualifications or impending results

2. Your ambitions for the future

3. Your personality and attitude

4. Your ability and talents

5. Your financial situation

6. Where you live and where you could live?

QUALIFICATIONS

First of all, you may be limited to the training schemes on offer by the qualifications you already have. Some accountancy qualifications are aimed at graduates and if you don't have a degree or don't intend studying for one, they can be struck off the list. However, it is worth reading entry requirements of the institutes carefully as some offer other, non-degree ways of getting a chartered qualification, the AAT Fast track route provided by the ICAEW, for example. Don't be afraid to call or email the institutes for advice on entry requirements to clarify what's required.

If you don't have exactly what the institute is looking for there may be ways around it by:

● Obtaining further qualifications before you apply

● Applying to the institute for any unlisted qualifications you have or exams you have sat to be considered

● Asking for any practical, work-related knowledge or experience to be considered.

Starting out with GCSEs or NVQs may mean that it takes a little longer to obtain the professional qualification you want, but it doesn't exclude you from working towards it. Look at the AAT syllabus as a starting point and go to your local Further Education College for advice on courses that can bump up your CV.

AMBITIONS

Ambitions for a particular career and aspirations for a future lifestyle are great to have. Those with focus and determination have every chance of achieving their goals, but those goals must be realistic.

Accountancy is rather like law, in that it requires continuous learning and a whole lot of studying before you even qualify. If you are 16 and are considering a career as a qualified accountant, you may not have those chartered letters after your name until you are at least 24. That's a minimum of eight years of learning and on-the-job training.

PERSONALITY

As we've mentioned above, it can be a long haul to accountancy, even if you are not aiming for chartered status. You need to be realistic about your chances of achieving your goals. Have you got the staying power? Realising that you may not be able to get to the end of a long slog of studying and working does not mean you haven't got what it takes. We are all different and some personalities are just not perfectly suited to a career in accountancy.

Accountancy involves:

- A lot of detailed work and learning

- Being confident with people and confident in the knowledge you have at your fingertips

- Judgement on just how much you can advise on in a climate of increased restrictions and regulation

- Stamina to cope with long hours and work stress

- Being comfortable with working on your own and taking important decisions as well as sharing projects with team members.

ABILITIES

Throughout this book accountants have emphasised the point that accountancy is no longer just a number-crunching game and that other talents and abilities are important. However, those without any ability to work with figures will find it very difficult to tackle the basics of accountancy. Outstanding mathematical skills are not necessary, but what is important is confidence with numbers and the ability to recognise when figures are just plain wrong. If maths is definitely your very worst subject, think again. Not only will you struggle with accountancy, but you're also unlikely to enjoy the experience.

Similarly, everyone has emphasised the need for good communication skills. As report-writing and presentation-giving are likely to be key parts of the job, you need to be confident with (and competent at) written and spoken communication.

FINANCIAL SITUATION

Accountancy can offer good prospects at senior level – especially in practice and in the City – but before that you may spend three to ten years on a trainee's wages. Chartered trainees earn between £11,000 and £16,000, while a newly qualified accountant can expect to earn between £20,000 and £30,000. These figures take into account differing employers, specialisms and geographical areas.

Careful planning and realistic thinking are required when looking at job and training opportunities from a financial point of view. Can you afford to live on a trainee's wage well into your mid-20s? Can you afford to run a car, have a social life, go on holiday? Can you afford to pay back student loans as well as work and train?

LOCATION

Where you live can have a big impact on your finances. Jobs in the South-East may pay more (with London weighting, for instance) but accommodation and transport costs may wipe out any extra in your wage packet. Before the attraction of the bright lights leads you to London, work out carefully how much you'll have coming in and how much you'll have to spend on the privilege of living in the capital.

Location isn't only about money, it's about support structure too. A trainee accountant's life is hard work and often highly stressed. You may feel the need to have friends and family around to give you moral and practical support while you're studying and working.

Those are the main factors to consider when looking at training and working opportunities. Some points may be more important to you than others, but it's wise to have sorted out most of them – in your head at least – before making any real decisions about your future.

GETTING THE MOST OUT OF TRAINING

Continuous education for us all – at whatever age or level – is becoming imperative if we want to progress in our career. Becoming an accountancy trainee is just the first step in what will be lifelong learning. Starting the right course at the right entry point with the right attitude is vital if it is to contribute to a trainee's self-esteem as well as the chances of success at work.

Training doesn't stop at chartered status. Historically once you had acquired the qualification, that was it, now institute members commit to Continued Professional Development. We've seen how important it is to keep up to date – not just in accountancy, but also in management and business areas.
Robert Jelly, Director of Education, CIMA

In order to get the most out of training everyone needs to look further than the syllabus, entry requirements, possible outcomes and general status of a selected course. A little homework is required.

First of all, imagine you are paying for your own training. It is likely that a sponsoring employer will pay for accountancy training and exams as well as provide days off for study leave, but nothing focuses the mind like having to pay good money for something you want to get good results from!

Once you have added up the full cost of study – over three, five or even ten years – think about how you are going to get value out of your investment. Consider the following steps:

1. Spend your time and effort on the training that gets you where you want to be. Family and friends, as well as an employer, can pile on the pressure when they think they know what's best for you. Be firm, because you know what you can do and, importantly, what you want to do. It's not enough to embark on a training course because you think it might be good, or others have told you it will be good for you: you have to want to do it, be interested in doing it and be determined to see it through to the finish. Only you know if it's realistically achievable.

2. If you think you've found the right course, write down what you want to achieve from it. You could divide your list into short-term and long-term goals. Make sure you understand fully what the course has to offer and match it with what you want to get out of it. They need to be compatible.

3. Once you have your list(s), write down how you will assess whether you have achieved your goals. For instance, will exams test your knowledge? Will you end up working in a different way? Will your employer notice improvements? Will you interact with people differently? Will you get a pay rise? Will you get a promotion? Will your confidence improve? Write down the relevant criteria next to the points on your list(s).

4. In completing the above, what you have prepared is a plan. In order to make sure you are achieving according to plan, you need to assess yourself at certain points in your training. After six months of training look at your plan and decide whether it is still appropriate, whether you are up to where you thought you'd be, and whether you want the same as you

did at the outset. If any of the answers to the above are negative, you might need to think again about your priorities and aspirations.

5. So that you don't get bogged down in your training – especially if it continues for years – approach it in small chunks. At the end of each training or study session, make a quick note of what you learnt that was new, what you learnt that was useful and anything you didn't quite understand. Go back to these notes before the next session and try to find out more about the learning points or ask someone who is more knowledgeable than you.

6. You can learn as much – if not more – from people as from books, CDs and the Internet. If you are training with people from different organisations, functions or levels to you, make contact with them and talk about the coursework. Networking is an invaluable tool for progression.

7. Finally, keep thinking how you can use what you have learnt. How will you apply the theory you have learnt? How will you change the way you work in response to what you have learnt? Try out your new skills and knowledge as you go along.

CHAPTER 10

What else is there?

By now, you should have a clearer picture of the accountant's job. It may be that you have a burning desire to begin accountancy training, or perhaps you are unsure.

Most people are attracted to a profession by what they believe it represents, but perception is not always reality. If you thought accountancy was all about adding up figures in the quiet of an office corner, think again. If you thought accountancy was all about earning high salaries and having lots of power, think again.

The audit is the end of the supply chain of accounting information. It is a look at the past, not the future. Nowadays accountants are much more involved in everything that leads up to the audit.
Robert Jelly, Director of Education, CIMA

If you are still confused, look back at the chapters at the beginning of this book, especially Chapters 4 and 5, to get a clearer picture of what an accountant's life is really like. If the attraction of accountancy is fading, read on for other career options related in various ways to accountancy. You may find something that sounds more 'you'. You can find out more about the professions below by contacting the organisations listed after each entry.

ALTERNATIVES TO ACCOUNTANCY

- If you are mathematically minded, prefer desk work to client relations, and want to work in finance and the public sector, go to Actuary

- If you are numerate, have a competitive instinct, are confident working with people at a high level, like solving problems, and want to work in commerce, go to Corporate Banking

- If you are numerate and enjoy academic research and putting theories into practice, go to Economist

- If you like solving problems and helping people, often in difficult circumstances, and don't mind a lot of paperwork, go to Insurance

- If you are numerate, enjoy risk-taking and practical problem-solving, like working with a variety of people every day, and want to work in business, go to Purchasing and Supply

- If you enjoy responsibility, have the ability to sum up people and situations, have good judgement and common sense and would like to work in the public sector, go to Tax Inspector.

ACTUARY
An actuary is primarily a statistician working in the insurance and finance sector. Actuaries use the theory of probability and the theory of compound interest together with statistical techniques to solve financial problems, suggest appropriate courses of action and predict the financial implications of such action.

The work is mathematical and half of all actuaries work in insurance on the technical side of life assurance and pension funds. In accident, fire and motor insurance actuaries assess risk and look at variables. Actuaries also work in banks, the Stock Exchange and government departments, but almost a third work in consultancy. There are limited opportunities in commerce or industry.

Almost all actuaries are graduates with a degree in a mathematical subject. Graduates require work experience and three to five years' study to qualify.

Actuaries need: specific talents and skills in mathematical and statistical analysis; the ability to solve complex problems; an analytical and inquisitive brain; and a liking for concentrated desk work.

Further information: Institute of Actuaries, Napier House, 4 Worcester Street, Gloucester Green, Oxford OX1 2AW, www.actuaries.org.uk.

CORPORATE BANKING
The more complex work on corporate banking is done in the corporate divisions of clearing banks and investment banks. Banks differ in the services they offer corporate clients; these services can range from transferring funds and lending money to advising on mergers and acquisitions or corporate finance. The larger investment and clearing banks' roles are changing and accountancy firms are increasingly muscling in on their business. Therefore, there is more crossover of roles, staff and interests than ever before.

People are required to perform different roles at different levels within the banks. Analysis is at the top of the scale, with entry-level jobs often being in sales. The most renowned job in this area is as a Dealer, a high-risk role that has declined in recent years. Bankers and corporate financiers are graduates, but Dealers are often support staff who make their own way in the bank. Experience gained in a specialist area in a bank can lead to movement between banks and into industry – and vice versa.

Banks are not taking as many trainees and graduates as they were in the 1980s and 1990s, but for those who work their way up the organisation, the financial rewards and status can be high.

A banker needs: to be a team-player; confidence to work at a high level; intelligence and flair; competitive drive; an analytical mind; practical problem-solving abilities and flexibility.

Further information: Chartered Institute of Bankers in Scotland, Drumsheugh House, 38b Drumsheugh Gardens, Edinburgh EH3 7SW. Tel: 0131 473 7777. Fax: 0131 473 7788. Email: info@ciobs.org.uk. www.ciobs.org.uk

London Investment Banking Association, 6 Frederick's Place, London EC2R 8BT. Tel: 020 7796 3606. Fax: 020 7796 4345. Email: liba@liba.org.uk. www.liba.org.uk

ECONOMIST

Economics comes under Social Sciences but is not actually regarded as a science. There is a variety of schools of thought, but economists base their work on judgements, testing out particular theories in practice.

Economists work in a variety of environments – town planning, industry, commerce, the City, financial and industrial journalism, trade unions, management consultancies, development programmes, and (the largest employer) the Civil Service.

Some economists work in specific areas of industry, while others develop specialist knowledge in areas such as environmental impact, traffic control, services for the disabled, higher education, health or public housing.

The role of the economist is one of adviser; decisions are made and implemented by other team members.

Economists study Economics at university but many Economics degrees can be combined with Business, Management, Computing or Accountancy to provide a range of specialisms. The basics of macro- and micro-economics will always be studied, along with an increasing emphasis on quantitative methods.

Economists need: numeracy and an analytical mind are essential for this career. It also helps to be thick-skinned and have a positive attitude, as theories can be proven wrong and people don't always take an economist's advice.

Further information: universities or university guides **(see Chapter 11)** for course details and career options.

INSURANCE

Insurance is fundamentally the compensation of losses arising from misfortunes – from a ship sinking or the abandonment of a major event, to replacing a video from a house burglary or compensating for a stolen car. The system works because people pay insurance but don't necessarily claim on it. The insurance equation is based on an important assessment of risk.

There are various roles in insurance:

- Underwriters assess risks, decide on insurability and how much it's going to cost. These people may also be called Insurance Surveyors. Some are Chartered Surveyors, but many aren't and have been are trained internally. Science and technology graduates also enter this side of the insurance business.

- Claims Staff assess the loss and determine the amount to be paid in the event of compensation. Sometimes independent Loss Adjustors are employed as specialists to do this job.

- Inspectors (sales agents) obtain new business and ensure existing customers are adequately covered.

- Insurance Brokers bring together those who want to be insured with the insurer. They find the best deals and most appropriate cover for their customers. Some brokers specialise in particular areas of insurance, e.g. marine brokers.

Most training for the above roles is work-based. Increasingly insurance companies look for graduates to train but there are opportunities for those with BTEC and A-level qualifications. Those with GCSEs may find training vacancies but these are becoming scarcer at the larger companies.

Insurance employees need: some mathematical and problem-solving ability; tact and diplomacy; good communication and negotiation skills.

Further information: Careers Information Officer, The Chartered
Insurance Institute, 20 Aldermanbury, London EC2V 7HY.
Customer Service Centre, CII, 42-48 High Road, South Woodford,
London E18 2JP. Tel: 020 8989 8464. Fax: 020 830 3052.
Email: customerserv@cii.co.uk. www.cii.co.uk

PURCHASING AND SUPPLY
Purchasing and supply covers the business of managing materials
in an organisation, and employees work in industry and the public
sector.

There are various roles in Purchasing and Supply:

● Planners ensure supplies of materials, tools, components and
  equipment to the organisation so it can function effectively

● Buyers seek out the providers of these supplies and negotiate
  contracts detailing quantity, quality, specification and delivery

● Purchasing Managers are in charge of stores management and
  inventory control.

Purchasing and Supply is needed for all sorts of organisations
and sometimes specific technical knowledge is required for
specialist industries. Also, with larger, international organisations
a second or third language is essential when dealing with foreign
suppliers.

Qualifications can be achieved at any level and school-leavers up
to postgraduates can enter the professional part-time courses.
Almost a third of entrants are over 30 years old, with many
employees using previous experience in business and
management to enter Purchasing and Supply. This is a growing
area of industry with increasing job opportunities, reflected in the
development of NVQs and SVQs in the subject.

Purchasing and Supply employees need: a head for figures; an
interest in business; good negotiating and interpersonal skills; to
be team players; a practical approach to problem-solving; an
awareness of international changes in the economy and
technology; and no aversion to risk-taking!

Further information: Chartered Institute of Purchasing and Supply, Easton House, Easton-on-the-Hill, Stamford, Lincs PE9 3NZ. Tel: 01780 756777. Fax: 01780 751610. www.cips.org

TAX INSPECTOR

Tax inspectors work for the Inland Revenue. Although most tax inspectors are civil servants, there are tax specialists who work on a consultancy basis for industry and commerce and who have an Inland Revenue background.

The main function of a Tax Inspector is to scrutinise a business's profit for tax purposes and work out what is owing in a tax year. By examining accounts and interviewing clients, the objective is to identify fraud or tax evasion. In addition, tax inspectors advise taxpayers on tax and business law.

Tax Inspectors are graduates who have completed a three-year professional qualification. Each year the Inland Revenue employs students with good degrees to train with the department. Some graduates, or those with BTEC or A-level qualifications will start as a Tax Officer – Executive Officer Civil Servant level – and will train on the job.

Tax Inspectors need: self-confidence; good judgement; good communication skills; attention to detail; administrative ability; and impartiality.

Further information: Civil Service Careers, Units 2-4 Lescren Way, Avonmouth, Bristol BS11 8DG. www.civil-service.gov.uk/jobs. www.ukonline.gov.uk for central government information and vacancies.

CHAPTER 11

Accountancy conclusions

As we've established over the last ten chapters, the accountancy profession has distinct advantages and may be the ideal career for some people.

Although an increasing number of young people are attracted to accountancy, it hasn't always been top of the careers list. Research has shown that most accountants arrived at their jobs by a circuitous route, rather than by design. This may be because accountancy has suffered from a poor public image, misinformation, and a lack of understanding.

Many accountants who started on this career path did so by accident – having worked in another area of industry or commerce – or took to accountancy after a complete change in career. Today it has an older age profile than many other professions, partly due to these factors, but also because most people enter the profession after the age of 21 and go on to train for a minimum of three years.

Nowadays accountancy is a much more alluring career, and prized training places and jobs are hard-won.

Accountants have become a whole lot more interesting. Although a very public disaster for the profession, Enron has made accountancy seem sexy. The larger profile of accountancy has helped people to understand more about the job we do. In fact, we've had an increase in applicants since accountancy hit the headlines. People started to realise we're not so boring after all!
Stevan Rolls, Director of Resourcing and Employee Integration, Ernst & Young

The increasing popularity is well overdue as accountancy has always had points in its favour – secure, well-paid, increasingly interesting employment, with varied and international job opportunities. These factors (in a time of economic uncertainty) make it a career to consider, but it is not necessarily suitable for everyone who's attracted to it.

DID YOU KNOW?
Membership in the UK and the Republic of Ireland of each of the accountancy bodies has increased every year from 1996 to 2001. (Key Facts and Trends in the Accountancy Profession 2002)

No matter how flexible, inclusive or available training and work-based learning becomes, accountancy will always remain an academic subject requiring concentration, determination and ability. There are no short cuts to success for those who aspire to senior positions with salaries to match.

There are, however, increased opportunities for those who don't want to be career accountants but who are interested in accountancy as a basis for a career. Determining which of these paths is the one that fits best is important early on, as the type of training and work environment will differ.

Of course, once you have made your initial decision, a change of direction is still possible, but you need to be aware (and be honest with yourself) just how dedicated you really are to the quest for the top job. It means continuous study, social and domestic sacrifices, long working hours and a degree of formality and responsibility that not everyone is comfortable with.

Those who enjoy solving problems and negotiating with colleagues and clients, have a fascination for the intricacies and vagaries of business and are prepared to make a lifelong learning commitment, have every chance of making it in accountancy – and enjoying the experience.

WHAT TO DO NEXT

The details, opinions and advice contained in this book are only a guide, designed to give those pondering a career in accountancy more information on which to base a decision to investigate further.

By now you may have decided:

● Accountancy is not for you

● Bookkeeping is a better career

● You want to look at a specific area of accountancy in a particular work environment

● Accountancy is a step towards entrepreneurship

● Accountancy knowledge is a useful stepping-stone for progression in a different corporate function.

The choice of courses, are numerous, and can be confusing. This book sets out to give you the tools to pinpoint the right information and sources, as well as read between the lines. Look at the facts, figures and quotes in the book and follow up any leads for further information.

Investigate the institute websites, make comparisons, ask questions and find people with first-hand experience to talk to for an insider's view. Don't forget, the six institutes are highly competitive – don't take all the gloss and marketing at face value. You need to make the right choice for you. Whichever path you take has to fit in with your personality, your ability, your aims and aspirations, and your lifestyle.

DID YOU KNOW?
The most rapidly growing accountancy bodies in terms of members in the UK and the Republic of Ireland since 1996 are ACCA (8.8% on an annual average basis), CIMA (5.6%) and ICAI (5.0%). (Key Facts and Trends in the Accountancy Profession 2002)

SIGNPOSTS

Below are some starting points for gathering information. Make use of the Internet and the library. If you don't have access to a careers or college library, career guides and reference books can be ordered from local or county libraries for just 70 pence. The books listed below can be bought from all major bookshops.

BACKGROUND
Accountancy Age magazine
This is the profession's main independent publication. The website carries news, previous features and press releases, all useful for background and research. It also has an extensive vacancies section.
www.accountancyage.com

INSTITUTES
ACCA
Association of Chartered Certified Accountants,
64 Finnieston Square, Glasgow G3 8DT
Tel: 0141 582 2000
Fax: 0141 582 2222
www.accaglobal.com
For general enquiries, contact info@accaglobal.com
For student enquiries contact students@accaglobal.com
ACCA CONNECT telephones are manned six days a week, Sunday to Friday.

www.accountingweb.co.uk is the ACCA-sponsored vacancies
website.

ICAEW
Institute of Chartered Accountants of England and Wales
postal address:
Chartered Accountants' Hall, PO Box 433, London EC2P 2BJ
Tel: 020 7920 8100. Fax: 020 7920 0547

Institute of Chartered Accountants of England and Wales,
Education and Training, Gloucester House, 399 Silbury Boulevard,
Central Milton Keynes, Bucks MK9 2HL
www.icaew.co.uk

For information on the ACA qualification:
Tel: 01908 248040. Email: careers@icaew.co.uk

ICAS
Institute of Chartered Accountants of Scotland,
CA House, 21 Haymarket Yard, Edinburgh EH12 5BH
Tel: 0131 347 0100. Fax: 0131 347 0105.
Student education fax: 0131 347 0108
www.icas.org.uk

ICAI
Institute of Chartered Accountants in Ireland,
Dublin office tel: 01 637 7200. Fax: 01 668 0842
Belfast office tel: 02890 230071. Fax: 02890 230071
www.icai.ie
career information from:
www.go-far.ie

CIMA
The Chartered Institute of Management Accountants
26 Chapter Street, London SW1P 4NP
Tel: 020 7663 5441. Fax: 020 7663 5442
www.cimaglobal.com

Training information from:
Email cima.training@cimaglobal.com
Tel: 020 8849 2434. Fax: 020 8849 2451

CIPFA
The Chartered Institute of Public Finance and Accountancy
3 Robert Street, London WC2N 6RL
Tel: 020 7543 5600. Fax: 020 7543 5700
Email: choices_info@cipfa.org
www.cipfa.org.uk

AAT
Association of Accounting Technicians
154 Clerkenwell Road, London EC1R 5AD
Tel: 020 7837 8600. Fax: 020 7837 8600
Email: aat@aat.org.uk
www.aat.co.uk
Student information from:
studentservices@aat.org.uk

TRADE UNIONS
UNIFI
UNIFI is Europe's largest specialist finance sector trade union,
with 158,000 members working for over 400 employers.

UNIFI, Sheffield House, 1b Amity Grove, Raynes Park, London
SW20 0LG
Tel: 020 8946 9151 Fax: 020 8879 7916   Minicom: 020 8944 5327

UNIFI, Oathall House, Oathall Road, Haywards Heath, West Sussex
RH16 3DG Tel: 01444 419119   Fax: 01444 416248
www.unifi.org.uk

PCS
The Public and Commercial Services Union is one of the UK's
largest trade unions. Its 288,000 members deliver governmental
services in both the public and private sectors. Members work in
government departments, agencies, public bodes, and in some
private companies, particularly in information technology.

The Public and Commercial Services Union, 160 Falcon Road,
London SW11 2LN. Tel: 020 7924 2727. Fax: 020 7924 1847.
www.pcs.org.uk

GENERAL CAREERS INFORMATION
www.insidecareers.co.uk
www.worktrain.gov.uk
www.connexions.gov.uk
www.connexionscard.com

The Penguin Careers Guide (2002) by Jan Widmer

TROTMAN BOOKS
Degree Course Offers: 2004 Entry (34th edition) by Brian Heap

Directory of University and College Entry 2004–2005 (DUCE) (9th edition)

UCAS/Trotman Complete Guide to Business Courses 2004

Choosing Your Degree Course and University (8th edition) by Brian Heap

The Student Book by Klaus Boehm and Jenny Lees-Spalding

Getting Into Business and Management Courses (5th edition)

Accountancy (Questions and Answers series*)*

Studying Business and Management (Questions and Answers series)